The Soviet Brigade in Cuba

DAVID D. NEWSOM

The Soviet Brigade in Cuba *A Study in Political Diplomacy*

Foreword by Admiral Stansfield Turner, USN (Ret.)

Published for the
Institute for the Study of Diplomacy,
Georgetown University

Indiana University Press   BLOOMINGTON AND INDIANAPOLIS

No part of this book may be reproduced or utilized in any form
or by any means, electronic or mechanical, including photocopying
and recording, or by any information storage and retrieval system,
without permission in writing from the publisher. The Association
of American University Presses' Resolution on Permissions constitutes
the only exception to this prohibition.

MANUFACTURED IN THE UNITED STATES OF AMERICA

Library of Congress Cataloging-in-Publication Data

Newsom, David D.
    The Soviet brigade in Cuba.

    1. United States—Foreign relations—1977–1981.
2. United States—Foreign relations—Soviet Union.
3. Soviet Union—Foreign relations—United States.
4. United States—Foreign relations—Cuba. 5. Cuba—
Foreign relations—United States. I. Title.
E872.N48   1987   327.73   86–45943
ISBN 0–253–35404–8
ISBN 0–253–20429–1 (pbk.)

1 2 3 4 5 91 90 89 88 87

CONTENTS

FOREWORD, Stansfield Turner   vii

PREFACE   xv

1. U.S. Diplomacy and Politics   1
2. August 1979: A Time of Testing   7
3. Cuba—An Emotional Issue   10
4. The Use and Misuse of Intelligence   18
5. U.S.-Soviet Understandings   23
6. Informing Congress and the Soviets   30
7. Managing the Issue   37
8. Conclusion   50

APPENDIXES
A. Daily Press Briefing, Department of State, August 31, 1979   60
B. Vance Press Conference, September 5, 1979   67
C. Remarks by Zbigniew Brzezinski to Out-of-Town Editors, Septem-   77
   ber 7, 1979
D. President Carter's TV Remarks, September 7, 1979   79
E. Carter Speech to the Nation, October 1, 1979   81
F. Background on the Question of the Soviet Troops in Cuba, De-   87
   partment of State Press Release, October 1, 1979
G. Letter from President Carter to Senator Stone, January 27, 1978   94
H. Letter from Secretary Vance to Senator Stone, July 27, 1979   96
I. Statements by President Kennedy, September 4 and 13, 1962 and   98
   January 24, 1963
J. Khrushchev and Kennedy Messages, October 27 and 28, 1962   102
NOTES   119

FOREWORD

Admiral Stansfield Turner, U.S.N. (ret.)
Former U.S. Director of Central Intelligence

Ambassador David Newsom has written a very readable and useful account of the diplomatic incident in 1979 when the United States accused the Soviet Union of having a "combat" brigade in Cuba. This is an event well worth studying and Ambassador Newsom is just the man to explain it to us. Not only was he a key participant in the incident and has researched it thoroughly, but in his lifetime he has seen American diplomacy from top to bottom. Having started at the lowest rungs of the Foreign Service ladder, he rose by 1979 to be the top career official in the State Department. In the course of his career in the Foreign Service, he witnessed many influences on American foreign policy. He explores two of them in this essay because they figured so prominently in the incident. One is the misuse of intelligence data; the other is the domestic political fortunes of some key members of Congress.

As a fellow participant in this crisis, I was there at the very beginning. That was in March 1979 when Zbigniew Brzezinski, National Security Advisor to the President, requested that the intelligence community review what we knew about the presence of Soviet military forces in Cuba. Usually when Brzezinski sent me a request for specific research like this it was because someone inside one of the intelligence organizations had seen some secret data and drawn a conclusion that he couldn't get his superiors to accept. He would feed it to Brzezinski's staff. If the conclusion fitted with the Brzezinski view of the world, they would urge him to push me to investigate it. I do not know if that is what occurred in this instance or whether it was just Brzezinski's own instincts. In either event, there really wasn't anything new going on in Cuba, but in finding that out, we in the intelligence community committed some serious errors.

As Ambassador Newsom recounts, out of the review that we conducted came a report from the National Security Agency in mid-July. It said that there was a Soviet "combat" brigade in Cuba. Until then the only Soviet military forces our intelligence reported as being in Cuba were labeled training units, neither brigades nor combat-oriented. The key point that Newsom makes is that the NSA's decision to use the term "combat" was not based on hard factual evidence. When the NSA found materials in its files that referred to a Soviet brigade, it drew an inference that it had a combat mission. It was an inference that proved to be critical. That the NSA should have made it raises questions about the responsibilities of the different organizations that conduct intelligence for our country, referred to collectively as the Intelligence Community.

Within that community there are two kinds of activities: collecting data and interpreting that data. Some of our intelligence agencies do one, some the other, and some both. The NSA is an agency only for collecting signals intelligence—information gleaned from radio, telephone, radar, and other electronic signals. Its job is to pass the data it gathers to the various agencies that do interpretation. Here, though, the NSA had clearly interpreted what it had collected, not just reported the factual data it had found. Of course, the line between collecting and interpreting data can be a fine one. The NSA must interpret what it collects just enough to know to whom to pass it for interpretation, to know whether it goes to the agencies that specialize in economic intelligence, or military, or whatever. The NSA also needs to do sufficient interpretation of what it collects to plan what to look for next; that is, if it intercepts a message that says a war is going to start tomorrow in Ruritania, it will want to focus its efforts in that area. That degree of interpretation is termed "processing," and it is an accepted activity for a collection agency to undertake. The NSA, however, habitually stretches its authority to process data and goes into full-scale interpretation of it.

That cuts into the role of the three principal interpretive, or analytic, agencies of the intelligence community: a branch of the CIA, the Defense Intelligence Agency, and the Bureau of Intelligence and Research in the State Department. There are good reasons why interpretation should be limited to these agencies and not include those for collection. First, when the analytic agencies interpret data they do so with the benefit of information gathered by all of the collection agencies, not just one. When a collection agency gets into interpretation, it is bound to be heavily influenced by the type of intelligence it collects. In this case that was signals intelligence, and there were certainly other important data available about Soviet activities in Cuba. Second, collection agencies may not have stored away all the background information relevant to a particular subject. That is not their responsibility nor are they equipped to do it. In this case, the whole record of what was agreed to between the United States and the Soviet Union during the Cuban missile crisis of 1962 was relevant information that a collection agency would not have had. Finally, the collection agencies are at a disadvantage in interpretation because they do not communicate regularly with the intelligence community's customers, the policymakers. The analytic agencies are supposed to do that in order to keep abreast of what the policymakers want and need to know about. In this case, for instance, the term "combat" touched a lot of nerves in policy councils by bringing to memory the Cuban missile crisis of 1962, but the NSA was not sensitive to that use of the term.

Why would the NSA stretch the bounds of its writ by interpreting this brigade as being a combat unit? Because it is the largest single agency in the intelligence community; a top command for some general or admiral; and a proud, highly competent organization that does not like to keep its light under a bushel. On top of that, being located halfway to Baltimore from Washington, D.C., it is a pretty remote member of the community. That physical remoteness is compounded by the fact that the NSA deals in such highly secret materials that it is often reluctant to share them with others lest a leak spoil their ability to get that kind of information again. It is a loner organization.

The NSA also has taken advantage of the fact that it works for two people, the Director of Central Intelligence and the Secretary of Defense. The Director has the authority to "task" the NSA—that is, to tell it what to collect—so that its efforts in collecting data can be harmonized with those of the agencies that take photographs and those that spy with human agents. The Secretary "manages" the NSA, that is, directs all its other activities. That responsibility rests with him largely because the NSA originated in the military and remains very important to military intelligence. The important issue is, where does "tasking" stop and "managing" begin? There is no clear line. Hence, neither the Director nor the Secretary exercises firm control over grey areas such as whether what the NSA is doing is interpretation or collection. The NSA understands this ambiguity and is skilled in taking advantage of it to do what it wants.

Still another question that the NSA's role in the combat brigade incident raises is that of how intelligence is distributed. In this case the NSA's interpretation that this was a combat unit was sent by it directly to its many customers, which include the White House. In theory the collection agencies should provide data only to the analytic agencies, who, in turn, would provide it to the customers along with their interpretation of it. That gives the customer the benefit of the opinion of the intelligence analysts who have the most background in these matters. Seldom is a piece of raw intelligence so conclusive that no interpretation is required. Yet, because some raw intelligence reports can be of urgent importance in a crisis, a practice has developed whereby all of our collection agencies distribute some of their reports directly to the customers, the policymakers.

Once the NSA's questionable interpretation that this was a combat brigade was widely circulated, an intelligence issue had turned into a diplomatic crisis. The NSA could have checked its view of whether the brigade in question deserved to be called a combat unit with one or another of the analytic agencies. It didn't do so, because the name of the game was getting credit for the scoop. The NSA had, in its view, an important report and couldn't resist being the first to get it on the street. Here, again, there was ambiguity over the role of the Director of Central Intelligence and that of the Secretary of Defense—that is, whether distribution falls under tasking or managing—and because these roles are unclear, the NSA does pretty much as it prefers.

The NSA's excursion into interpretation and its subsequent wide distribution of its conclusion were the genesis of this crisis over a Soviet brigade in Cuba; but the rest of the intelligence community did not perform any better. When the analytic agencies did receive the NSA's report, they failed to check it out carefully. Information that was available, including the fact that the Kennedy administration had understood that a Soviet brigade would remain in just the location of this unit, was not immediately uncovered. The community gave its concurrence to the NSA's thesis well before more research revealed that there was not much new about this unit, no matter what one called it. In my view, the desultory response of the rest of the community was the obverse of the NSA's sense of exclusiveness and superiority. The other agencies, having been scooped, did not want to grace the NSA's report as being worthy of much attention. Finally, though, it became a *cause célèbre* and they were forced to dig into it. That is when all the data and interpretation came forward that said that whatever the Soviets had there, it was not anything new.

Both the lack of community attention to what the NSA had said and the NSA's unwillingness to remain within its assigned bounds reveal fundamental problems within our intelligence structure. When this sort of thing has happened in the past, the President has often given more authority to the Director of Central Intelligence. Thus, over the years since 1947, when we organized an intelligence community, there has been a progressive strengthening of the role of the Director as the leader of that community. The Soviet brigade affair raises legitimate questions as to whether additional centralization of authority over the community is in order. The argument can logically be made, for instance, that if the ambiguities in authority over the NSA were clarified, this sort of mishap might not happen again.

There are, though, good reasons to be hesitant about too much centralization. The primary one is that democracies have always been cautious about how much authority over secret intelligence they concentrate in one man's hands. Even if we are not worried about the potential for abuse of secret authority, we do need to worry about vesting in one man a great deal of authority over how we collect intelligence and what conclusions our intelligence analysts reach in interpreting it. If he happened to be wrong, the country could be in trouble. Thus, we are always up against a compromise between what would best help us avoid possible errors like the one over the Soviet brigade and what concentration of authority we think is prudent.

We should keep in mind that the case for central control over the collection agencies, where teamwork is essential and great expense or risk is involved, is more important than over the analytic agencies, where we deliberately foster competitive analyses to ensure that the best ideas are brought forward. I believe, then, that one of the lessons of the Soviet brigade fiasco is that the Director of Central Intelligence could be given enough additional authority over the NSA to curb the degree of independence it shows with regard to doing analysis and distributing its product.

The other fascinating aspect of Ambassador Newsom's study is the role of domestic politics in this crisis. Once the NSA's report had leaked, the concern of two senators over their reelection prospects turned it into a major issue. Each senator had reason to jump on this report of Soviet activity in Cuba to help him improve his standing with his electorate. In the process, the issue poisoned attitudes toward the pending SALT II treaty with the Soviets. A narrow window of opportunity for passage soon closed. Ambassador Newsom points out that there were some questionable decisions made as to how to handle this issue with the Senate and the public to try to save the SALT II treaty. He is by no means unwilling to lay out the pros and cons of those decisions, including the ones he made. The only place he seems to pull punches is in commenting on the fact that Zbigniew Brzezinski publicly inflamed this issue at the same time the Secretary of State was trying to damp it down. Strong differences between national security advisers and secretaries of state have, unfortunately, been all too common. This, though, is an excellent instance in which to note how much damage can be done thereby to the country and to a president.

One of the most trenchant conclusions in this study is that the U.S. government ended up importuning the Soviet government to offer us some concession that would placate U.S. domestic forces opposed to the SALT II treaty. The Soviets probably were not able to believe that our intelligence was so inept and assumed that we were up to no good. They refused to help out. Whether SALT II would have been ratified by the Senate if this artificial crisis had not occurred we will never know. We do know that this bizarre sequence of events did delay its consideration during a critical period. There were more than enough mistakes that put us into this plight and David Newsom's thorough and thoughtful review of them provides valuable food for thought to those interested in the workings of modern diplomacy.

PREFACE

In the fall of 1979 I was a participant, as Under Secretary of State for Political Affairs, in a bizarre episode of foreign policy decision making regarding the reported presence of a Soviet "combat" brigade in Cuba. The military unit involved, while insignificant in terms of the power balance in the Caribbean area, was given prominence by political and foreign policy considerations within the United States.

I have chosen to try to capture the details of that episode as a case history to illustrate the pressures and problems of the decision-making process in the United States and the impact of that process on U.S. diplomacy in a particularly critical period of global tension. Although a participant, I have written this case history in the third person; it is intended as a contribution to the understanding of the process, not as a memoir.

Much of the material on which I have drawn came from a review of my own official files, made available under standing arrangements with the Department of State.

Others have also written extensively on this episode; inevitably there will be some parallel recounting of the basic events and background.

Dr. Gloria Duffy, now president of Global Outlook in San Jose, published two studies—written primarily from the standpoint of the impact on U.S.-Soviet relations—while she was associated with the Arms Control and Disarmament Program at Stanford University. One, "Crisis Mangling and the Cuban Brigade," was published in *International Security*, Summer 1983.[1] A second, "Crisis Prevention in Cuba," was published as a chapter in a book, *Managing U.S.-Soviet Rivalry*, edited by Alexander L. George.[2] Dr. Duffy made available to me both of these manuscripts in addition to other as yet unpublished writing on the same incident. I have benefited from her insight and in some cases, appropriately noted, have drawn on her material.

Raymond Garthoff, former arms control official and ambassador to

Bulgaria, shared with me a chapter he wrote on the incident.[3] Former Secretary of State Cyrus Vance, former National Security Adviser Zbigniew Brzezinski, and former President Jimmy Carter all made references to it in their memoirs.[4] Donald Oberdorfer, of the *Washington Post*, published a lengthy postmortem on the incident that is largely consistent with my own recollections and with official files.[5]

I am indebted, particularly, to Admiral Stansfield Turner, who took time from a busy schedule to write the Foreword.

I sent drafts of the manuscript to all of the participants for their comments and many responded. I was particularly grateful for the helpful comments of Senator Frank Church given to me in a meeting with him some time before his untimely death.

Whatever the source of the material and comments, however, the conclusions are my own.

The preparation of this study has been assisted by a grant from the Exxon Education Foundation to the Institute for the Study of Diplomacy, Georgetown University.

The Soviet Brigade
in Cuba

ONE

U.S. Diplomacy
and Politics

To understand the diplomacy of any nation, it is essential to understand that nation: its history, the attitudes of its people, the nature of its institutions, and the various channels through which it communicates with others. This is especially true for the United States; in no other nation do domestic forces have a greater impact on the country's foreign relations.

In the United States, the study of diplomacy has tended to focus on how we negotiate with other countries. The study of the internal foreign policy-making process and its relationship to domestic institutions and pressures has been regarded as a separate field, even though the two are closely and intimately related.

In a sense, the decision-making process in the United States never ends. Those who lose out in an internal debate may—and often do—continue to press their case throughout the period of diplomatic negotiation. Opponents of earlier decisions may also choose to exploit the domestic political process; the division between executive and legislative powers and the processes of Senate ratification of treaties and congressional review of agreements unique to the United States give opponents extraordinary leverage. The free play of the press and of domestic pressure groups adds further complication.

American diplomacy is thus at the mercy of these internal processes. The twists and turns of policy, which often seem puzzling to those watching from outside, whether in the United States or abroad, can largely be explained by the nature of the process. Changing circumstances, efforts to change policies, and sudden unauthorized disclosures can alter the fate of diplomatic efforts even after agreements may have been reached in official discussions with other countries.

American diplomats have often found that one of their primary and most difficult tasks is to explain this phenomenon to those across the negotiating table. Highly centralized and nondemocratic countries rarely have this problem. Even in parliamentary democracies, the problem is minimized because there is no separation of executive and legislative powers. There exists, too, in most European countries a recognition that "the State" has certain powers in foreign relations which are not challenged once a governmental decision is made.

The management of official U.S. diplomacy is further marked by numerous official, semiofficial, and private channels through which attitudes are conveyed and relations maintained with individuals and institutions abroad. Even within the executive, the White House and the State Department can transmit different nuances to their counterparts abroad. The Departments of Defense, Treasury, Agriculture, Commerce, Justice, and Labor also have their respective opposites abroad with which relations are maintained.

Members of Congress have significant links with foreign groups. Unhampered by executive responsibility, they convey attitudes that are often markedly different from official U.S. policy. They collect intelligence that they may claim to be more accurate than that of the official agencies. The media reports the diversity of opinions and policies to every corner of the world. Special interest groups mount their own efforts to influence policies, abroad as well as at home. Many multinational corporations and major banks have established direct networks to foreign governments. The credibility of official diplomacy can be severely tested by views conveyed abroad through any one of these channels. In short, United States diplomacy is diplomacy in a goldfish bowl.

Few episodes have more dramatically illustrated this interlinking of domestic politics and diplomacy than the episode of the Soviet brigade in Cuba in 1979. The writing of those who observed this incident from the outside is almost universally critical of the manner in which it was handled. Such critics question how a relatively minor incident, trivial as a national security issue, could develop in a way that affected U.S.-Soviet relations and related events around the world. The impression of triviality was probably best noted in a comic strip comment that the best way to deal with the brigade was to "call out the Florida highway patrol."

Mistakes may have been made in the handling of each step in the episode. Different approaches might have been possible. To those involved, however, there was the sense of an inexorable progression of circumstances, dictated by political and bureaucratic responses to the unexpected in foreign policy. Decisions made at each step of the way, logical in the light of the objectives and circumstances of the moment, may have contributed to the exaggeration of a relatively minor event. The pressures of decision making give an immediacy to each decision that can cloud the wider perspective. This may be true in all governments. The complicated executive-legislative relationship and the vulnerability of all actions within the U.S. government to unexpected exposure, however, may make the American process more complicated.

The handling of the brigade episode described in subsequent chapters illustrates a number of basic and relatively constant factors in American decision making. These factors can be called weaknesses, but they are not easily changed. They have affected other decisions, as well as the decisions on the Soviet brigade.

Virtually every U.S. administration is, to some extent, a coalition of diverse elements. The Carter administration was no exception. The diversity was particularly apparent in questions relating to policies toward the Soviet Union. By 1979 the differences in point of view between Secretary Vance in the State Department and Dr. Brzezinski in the White House were apparent to all. The secretary believed that it was necessary to keep channels open to the Soviet Union and to govern rhetoric to minimize differences. Dr. Brzezinski saw Soviet actions as part of a wider global offensive and felt that it was both politically and strategically necessary for the administration to call public attention to the lack of Soviet sensitivity to U.S. interests around the world.

The differences embodied in the views of these two senior officials were reflected in both the organization and the attitudes of those below them in the National Security Council and the State Department. The organization of Soviet affairs in the State Department was divided bureaucratically, although not ideologically, between Marshall Shulman, special advisor to the secretary of state, and officers in the Bureau of European Affairs, who dealt with the normal day-to-day relationships with the Soviet Union. Dr. Shulman was, for critical subjects, the primary action officer for the secretary and was, with rare exceptions, entrusted by Secretary Vance to deal on major issues with the senior officials of the Soviet embassy. Shulman sat in on most meetings between Secretary Vance and Soviet Ambassador Anatoly Dobrynin.

Policy making toward the Soviet Union involved decisions not only on where responsibility would lie, but also on channels that would be used to communicate. Secretary Vance felt that the most valuable channel was through Ambassador Dobrynin, a member of the Central Committee of the Soviet Communist Party. The secretary felt that papers went through fewer hands and that Dobrynin, because of his long experience in Washington, was, perhaps, a better interpreter of the Washington scene. The American ambassador in Moscow, Malcolm Toon, was therefore largely left out of the circuit on critical events. This State Department arrangement, however, did not preclude occasional meetings between Dr. Brzezinski and Ambassador Dobrynin and other Soviets, not always with the immediate knowledge of the secretary of state.

Events surrounding the decisions on the Soviet brigade also illustrate the importance of words in both international diplomacy and domestic politics. As the account demonstrates, the use of certain words, such as "combat" in referring to the brigade, "status quo" in referring to the situation in Cuba, and "base" in correspondence with members of

Congress, created impressions and signals which, in themselves, became part of the problem.

Many of the circumstances in this episode revolved around the activities of members of the United States Senate. The episode illustrates not only the impact of legislative politics upon the executive, but also the interrelationship of foreign policy questions. Actions that may be taken on one issue frequently affect the attitudes and actions involving other problems. The responses of the two senators involved in the revelation of a Soviet brigade were undoubtedly affected by the actions that one had taken on the Panama Canal treaties and the other had taken on SALT II.

Those outside the United States, and especially in a totalitarian country such as the Soviet Union, must find the American system puzzling. Explanations that the Soviet brigade issue was brought about by internal politics and the exploitation of intelligence information were not credible to most observers outside the United States. The Soviets, in particular, suspected an ulterior motive and found it in what they believed was the desire of the administration to seek an excuse for backing away from the SALT treaty. The Soviets were deaf to suggestions that they might help the administration by adopting a cooperative attitude in resolving the brigade issue. If they believed that this was an internal U.S. political problem, which I doubt, they clearly felt that the price suggested to meet the vagaries of American internal politics was too high.

The episode also illustrated the lack of institutional memory within the U.S. government. Not only was it necessary to pull together and reevaluate the nature of the understandings with the Soviet Union reached as a result of the 1962 missile crisis, but it was also necessary to reexamine the nature of the commitments made under the Monroe Doctrine.[6] The most glaring failure of institutional memory was in the lack of any immediate process that would have reminded policymakers that some Soviet troops remained in Cuba after the withdrawal of the missiles in 1963.

Finally, a true evaluation of this event cannot be made without reference to the relatively lonely position of the secretary of state within the administration. While Secretary of State Vance remained always discreet about his relations with the rest of the administration, those around him could not help but sense uncertainty in his mind about the president's attitude toward him. His desire to demonstrate his leadership of the process may well have been a factor in his determination to resolve the Soviet brigade issue in a way that minimized damage to our foreign relations and to broader administration policy. His loneliness was no doubt aggravated by the fact that most senior officials, including the president, were away from Washington at the time these events were unfolding.

It was not as if the Soviet brigade were the only issue that the secretary was facing at that time. The summer of 1979 was an eventful one on the State Department's seventh floor. A full understanding of the brigade issue and of how it was handled is not possible without understanding all else that was happening in that particular period of U.S. history.

T W O

August 1979:
A Time of Testing

July and August of 1979 were busy months on the executive floor of the State Department. There was, first of all, SALT II. The second Strategic Arms Limitation Treaty with the Soviet Union had been initialed on April 18 and formally signed by President Carter and Secretary Brezhnev on June 18. The formal debate had begun before the Senate Foreign Relations Committee on July 9. The administration faced strong opposition in the Senate and among powerful interest groups and opinion makers even before the episode of the Soviet brigade in Cuba. The brigade episode came in the midst of a priority effort by the administration to garner support for the treaty.

Other events were also focusing attention on the Soviet-U.S. relationship. By 1979 the Carter administration was shifting from an emphasis on building relations with the Soviets to a stronger emphasis on U.S. defense. On June 8, President Carter had approved the plans to proceed with the MX missile. The administration was pressing for a higher level of defense spending. The Soviets saw this as a change in the earlier mood of the administration.

Relations were also strained by another incident. On August 27, there had been a prolonged and difficult negotiation at the Kennedy airport in New York between U.S. Ambassador Donald McHenry and Soviet officials over the departure of a Bolshoi dancer whose husband had defected within the United States.

There were problems in other foreign policy areas, too.

In January a revolution had occurred in Iran, ousting a close ally of the United States, the Shah of Iran. Domestically the response in some quarters was to attack the administration for failures of intelligence and for losing a significant ally in the Middle East. In addition, the revolution in Iran had placed the ratification of the Strategic Arms Limitation Agreement in further jeopardy: the loss of intelligence monitoring sites in Iran raised new questions concerning the problem of verification.

In April serious fighting had broken out in Nicaragua, forcing the departure on July 17 of President Anastasio Somoza. Many in the United States, conservatives in particular, regarded this as a setback for the United States and a gain for Cuba. Only one week after Somoza's departure, three leaders of the Nicaraguan junta had visited Cuba. The events in Nicaragua added to growing concern in the administration over Cuba's activities in the Caribbean basin and Central America. Earlier in the year, on March 13, Cuban influence in the Caribbean had been highlighted by the appearance of Cuban support for a leftist government that took over in Granada.

The conference of nonaligned nations was to open in Havana on September 3. The world's spotlight was on Cuba. It was clear from discussions between the United States and some nonaligned countries that there would be serious divisions at Havana between those countries favoring a genuinely nonaligned position on international issues and those countries closely allied with the Soviet Union. U.S. diplomacy was involved in seeking to encourage moderate governments of this grouping to oppose efforts both to oust Egypt from the movement and to recognize the Vietnam-supported regime in Kampuchea. The United States was particularly counting on Yugoslavia, Sri Lanka, and Indonesia. Additionally, talks on the future of Rhodesia-Zimbabwe were at a crucial stage in London; the United States was not a participant but had great interest in a satisfactory outcome.

Internal events also preoccupied those in leadership positions. The administration was itself emerging from events that had given a public impression of disarray at the senior levels of the executive. On July 19, President Carter had engineered a shake-up both of his cabinet and of his White House staff. On August 27, the U.S. ambassador to the United Nations, Andrew Young, had resigned following controversy over a meeting he had had with a representative of the Palestine Liberation Organization.

Senator Edward Kennedy was beginning to challenge President Carter for the Democratic nomination in 1980. The implementing legislation for the controversial Panama Canal treaties was facing a major battle in the House. The Panamanian flag was due to be hoisted in the Canal Zone October 1.

It was past the midpoint of the administration and tensions were rising over policy directions and among the various personalities. The atmosphere was affected by these pressures and a sense that while there had been successes, some very difficult problems lay ahead.

Those in office were also conscious of the vulnerability to public exposure of their deliberations and their differences. The leak, either to advance or to discredit a policy, and the resulting debate over which part of the administration had leaked the information had become part of the Washington scene. There were frequent references in the press and on TV to differences over policies toward the Soviets, Iran, and Nicaragua. When a new development occurred, it was natural that among the first considerations of the policymakers would be the possibility that it would be leaked, either by advocates or adversaries. This was likely to be particularly true with a development that touched on a controversial area such as Cuba.

THREE

Cuba—An Emotional Issue

Few issues are as emotionally charged in American foreign policy as those relating to Cuba. The substantial Soviet presence in an island ninety miles from our shores, and the realization by succeeding administrations of how limited is the capacity of the United States to contain Cuban activities, add an element of frustration to every issue involving Cuba.

The Carter administration took office in 1977 with the intention of improving relations with Cuba. An interests section was opened in the Swiss embassy in Havana, and discussions were initiated which resulted in some marginal improvements in communication between Cuba and the United States and in some release of prisoners.

Basic differences that existed between the United States and Cuba were aggravated by the presence in Africa of Cuban troops, seen as surrogates of the Soviet Union.

Two schools of thought existed within the administration. One wished to continue to improve bilateral relations. The other, centering largely in the White House, wanted to make a Cuban withdrawal from Africa a precondition to an improvement in bilateral relations. As time went by, the belief that Cuba was actively involved in Central American issues, such as the ouster of Somoza in Nicaragua, added to the reluctance of the administration to talk directly with the Cubans.

Whenever Cuba is brought up, it is natural that every president since Kennedy thinks of the Cuban missile crisis of 1962. A president resolves that, if there is ever another confrontation with the Soviet Union of that significance, he does not wish to seem any less skillful or less courageous than was President Kennedy in dealing with the problem. There has been a tendency, which showed itself again in the Soviet brigade crisis, to consider every development in Cuba a parallel to the missile crisis.

The Cuban missile crisis and the U.S.-Soviet understandings which followed were basic to the handling of all issues relating to the Soviet presence in the years that followed. Such questions were handled primarily as matters between the United States and the Soviet Union, with Cuba, more or less, as a bystander.

Cuban exiles in the United States, particularly in Florida, desirous of creating and sustaining a strong anti-Castro position in every administration, maintained pressure on administrations to take the Soviet presence seriously. The large Cuban exile population furnished to members of the Senate and to others in the federal government information that was intended to demonstrate that the Soviets and the Cubans were moving closer and closer together.

The episode of the Soviet brigade in Cuba began with a request by Dr. Brzezinski to the intelligence community to take a look at the Soviet presence in Cuba.[7] He was moved by a sense that the Soviet presence might be growing, and undoubtedly as well by a desire to demonstrate, within the councils of government, the basic threat to U.S. interests of the Soviet presence in the Caribbean.

Dr. Brzezinski's original request for more intelligence data was the starting point of the event; but the activities of two members of the United States Senate gave it its public prominence and national significance.

In the United States, members of Congress are basically representatives of individual constituencies. While they have an obligation to a national political party, the attitude of their constituents will determine whether they are reelected to the Congress. A fundamental conflict, therefore, exists in the activities of many senators between the views of that senator's district and the senator's responsibility to a national party or a national administration.

In the case of the Soviet brigade, the significance of the dilemma was heightened by the fact that both senators involved were Democrats, both were members of the Senate Committee on Foreign Relations, and one was its chairman.

Richard Bernard Stone, a Democrat of Tallahassee, Florida, was elected to the U.S. Senate in 1974. A *cum laude* graduate of Harvard with a degree from the Columbia University Law School, he had been the city attorney of Miami, a state senator, and Florida's secretary of state. Coming to the Senate, he received one of the coveted vacancies on the Foreign Relations Committee. Although Stone had had no significant international experience, he had two special interests in the field of foreign affairs: the Middle East and Cuba. He was given a seat on the Middle East subcommittee and, during the time he was in the Senate, his support was considered important to the administration on issues relating to the Middle East.

The interest of greatest political importance to him, however, was Cuba. Many of the anti-Castro exiles who fled Cuba in the early 1960s settled in Dade County, Florida. There they prospered and became both a financial and a political force in the Miami area and in the state. Senator Stone was close to this community, many of whom still had links to people in Cuba. He was open to their reports of both fact and rumor regarding events in Cuba and, in particular, Soviet activities on the island.

Senator Stone was well acquainted with the events surrounding the missile crisis of 1962, the subsequent understandings with the Soviets, and the further crisis over Soviet nuclear submarines in 1970. Because it was of interest to his constituents and, as such, was good politics, he followed closely and sought to trace every report of further Soviet moves on the island. Many reports came to him through his own informal network of Cubans. Others came through his contacts in the intelligence community. He was alert to reports on the harbor of Cienfuegos, where

Soviet submarines had called in 1970 and where, his informants told him, new buildings were being erected.

Senator Stone had been very much in the forefront of those pressing the State Department to respond to intelligence reports in mid-1978 on the delivery to Cuba of a new Soviet-built fighter-bomber aircraft, the MIG-23D. He raised the question of whether this was a violation of the earlier 1962 understandings with the Soviets on weapons systems in Cuba. After a detailed examination of the intelligence data, the administration replied that the new fighter, without a nuclear capacity, did not constitute a violation.

At about this same time Senator Stone had also written Secretary of State Vance referring to reports of more recent visits of Soviet submarines with nuclear weapons to Cuba and asking why such visits had not drawn a protest from the United States. In a clarification, the State Department took the position that the submarines came on port calls, which did not constitute a violation of the understandings with the Soviets.[8]

The ratification of the Panama Canal treaties in 1978 had posed special problems for Senator Stone. To his Cuban—as well as his conservative—constituents in Florida the treaties appeared to open the way for Cuban or Soviet control of this vital waterway. Sentiment ran strongly against any document lessening the U.S. presence and control.

In 1976, Stone had referred to Panama as a "left-leaning, rickety, tin-horn dictatorship" and vowed "never" to negotiate away the canal. Subsequently, he came to realize that defeat of the treaties would create serious problems in relations with the rest of Latin America, problems that "no amount of military force could suppress."[9]

In order to reconcile the earlier statement with this new understanding of the treaties, Stone sought a way to support the treaties without losing constituent backing. He thus requested from the president a reassurance that the United States planned no retreat from its military commitments in the Caribbean. Conversations with Hamilton Jordan, President Carter's chief of staff, produced a letter from the president to Stone dated January 27, 1978. This letter said that "ratification of the Panama Canal Treaties should not be viewed by any power as signaling a retreat by the United States in Latin America." The letter added, "In particular, it has been and will continue to be the policy of the United States to oppose any efforts, direct or indirect, by the Soviet Union to establish military bases in the Western Hemisphere."[10]

That letter, and the use of the word "bases" in particular, was to figure centrally in the subsequent discussion of the Soviet brigade. In a Florida press conference, Stone labeled the letter "a major policy statement" and said he would "in all likelihood" vote for the treaties. He emphasized that his decision was not political: if he were concerned about votes, "I'd vote against the treaties. That would be in line with the majority of my constituents."[11]

Lobbyists continued to pressure Stone to vote against the treaties and the subsequent implementing legislation. In April 1978, the American Conservative Union launched a three-day television advertising blitz over Florida stations, urging viewers to send telegrams to Stone and Lawton Chiles, Florida's other senator.[12]

Stone held firm and voted for the treaties, but in the ensuing months he was even more sensitive to reports of Soviet activities in Cuba. As the 1980 elections approached, he was also increasingly concerned about his local political standing.

Stone's vote on the Panama Canal treaties, the political requirement that he increase his vigilance on matters concerning Cuba, and his upcoming race in the 1980 elections combined to affect the way he approached the SALT II debate. It was, in large part, his need to assert skepticism with respect to Soviet behavior (including treaty compliance) that led to the public unraveling of the Soviet brigade story.

Stone's approach was to claim that these past events constituted violations of an agreement. SALT was similar to the 1962 understanding because it dealt with the deployment of nuclear weapons. If the Soviets could not be trusted to abide by the terms of the understandings on Cuba, how could they be trusted to agree to the terms of SALT II?[13]

This was the background when, on the morning of July 17, Senator Stone was handed a new cause. According to press reports, as Stone entered the Senate committee hearing room for an open hearing on SALT, he was informed, "from trusted sources," that there was a fully armed Soviet brigade based on Cuba. This brigade had apparently been, up to that point, undetected by U.S. intelligence. In a line of questioning directed to Admirals Thomas Moorer and Elmo Zumwalt, retired members of the Joint Chiefs of Staff, Senator Stone alluded to his possession of the intelligence.[14] During closed hearings held later in the day, he pressed Secretary of Defense Harold Brown to disclose more.

The secretary of defense responded that "there is no evidence of any substantial increase in the size of the Soviet military presence in Cuba over the past several years."[15] The chairman of the committee, Senator Frank Church of Idaho, and the ranking Republican, Jacob Javits of New York, issued a press release supporting Secretary Brown's statement.

Stone was not satisfied and he sought further comment from the secretary of state. Secretary of State Vance wrote to Stone on July 27, repeating the language of Secretary Brown. The correspondence with Senator Stone was an indication that, as in the case of the Panama Canal treaties, his vote on SALT was important.[16]

Shortly after public disclosure of a Soviet military presence in Cuba, the *Miami Herald* analyzed the events leading to the disclosure:

> If it can be accurately said that the Carter administration has gotten itself into a diplomatic box over the Russian troops in Cuba—and coincidentally over SALT II ratification—then it can also be accurately said that Florida's own junior Senator, Dick Stone, is the one who built the box.
>
> Stone's "carpentry" in this began almost by accident when, some say, he began looking for an angle of the SALT II debate that he could exploit to his political benefit in Florida.
>
> He needed to take a hard line in the hearings in order to compensate for his controversial decision a year ago in favor of the Panama Canal Treaties—a vote that lost him support among conservatives.
>
> That angle appeared to be Cuba. . . .[17]

A similar dilemma faced the other senator, Frank Church of Idaho, a Democrat, and chairman of the Senate Foreign Relations Committee. He, too, came from a conservative state where many were unsympathetic with the internationalist positions he often espoused. He also had a history of relations with Cuba. And he, too, was to run for reelection in 1980.

Church, a Phi Beta Kappa graduate of Stanford University with a degree from Stanford Law School, was first elected to the Senate in 1962. He achieved national prominence early in his senatorial career as the national Jaycee's outstanding young man. He was the keynoter at the Democratic National Convention in 1964. His name was frequently mentioned as a future candidate for president or vice president. Liberal in outlook, he was prominent in the passage of legislation placing greater restrictions on executive activity in foreign affairs following the Vietnam war. He was chairman of the Senate Select Committee that exposed many of the illegal activities of the Central Intelligence Agency.

In his leadership role on the Foreign Relations Committee, and despite the conservative opposition in his own state, Church was the floor manager in 1978 for the Panama Canal treaties. He argued that the rules established in the expansionist days of 1903 were long outdated. He said that the new treaties would secure better relations not only with Panama but also with Latin America generally. They would, he assured the Senate, protect U.S. interests in the canal. Opponents, he asserted, were on a "sentimental journey back to the era of Teddy Roosevelt, the big stick, and the Great White Fleet."[18]

Frank Church's internationalist outlook had received wide attention in April 1977 when, with the encouragement of the newly elected Carter administration, he had made a three-day visit to Cuba to explore with Fidel Castro the possibilities of better relations between the two countries. According to the *New York Times*, Church was concerned then about the political repercussions in his home state resulting from a widely publicized mission to help restore relations with a Communist nation.[19] His fears were confirmed when two and a half years later conservative political action committees opposing him in Idaho ran television ads using pictures of Castro and Church together.

On July 17, 1979, when Senator Stone asked Secretary Brown questions about a Soviet brigade in Cuba, Church must have recalled still another embarrassing involvement with Cuba. In 1962, when Mr. Church was in his first Senate reelection campaign, Senator Kenneth Keating, Republican of New York, claimed that the Soviets were placing nuclear missiles in Cuba. The Kennedy administration denied the charges. Church traveled to Guantánamo and returned to campaign in Idaho, denying Keating's claim. Within two months, reports of the missiles were confirmed.[20]

If Church recalled this incident, it did not deter him, in 1979, from once more supporting a Democratic administration in denying a report of Soviet activities in Cuba. The strength of his reaction to confirmation of the Soviet brigade may be laid to politics; it could also be laid to previous experience in supporting administrations on Cuba.

F O U R

———

The Use and Misuse
of Intelligence

If two senators were able to create an issue over a Soviet brigade in
Cuba, they were aided in doing so by the availability of intelligence
data. In the post–World War II years, as the sophistication of intelligence
methods increased, so did the pressure and the temptation to make use
of sensitive data. Inevitably, substantial information on intelligence
methods became available as well. President Kennedy used photographs
from the U-2 aircraft in discussing the presence of Soviet missiles in
Cuba. Information acquired by sensitive means was frequently used
publicly during the Vietnam war to justify and explain actions and
policies.

In the seventies, the hearings chaired by Frank Church on the actions
of the Central Intelligence Agency further exposed the capacities of the
intelligence community—and whetted the appetites of those in the Congress, the executive, and the media for more. By the late seventies,
sensitive intelligence was disseminated daily to a substantial number of
addressees in both the executive and the Congress. Having access became a status symbol. Members of Congress and enterprising reporters
established links with those in the intelligence agencies following their

particular interests. The intelligence leak became more a practice than a rarity, and the makers of foreign policy could effectively control neither the release nor the interpretation of intelligence.

Wider dissemination of and pressure to use intelligence meant that it often entered the public domain without full evaluation and before policies to deal with it had been established. Because intelligence is often partial or fragmented, its release can mislead; the account of the full circumstances may never catch up.

Despite a public perception to the contrary, intelligence gained by sophisticated methods can have serious limitations. Photos from the air may reveal equipment but they cannot necessarily reveal the nationality of the person operating it. The monitoring of voices may disclose the existence of a military unit but will not necessarily give details.

Intelligence on Cuba was largely technical. Because it depended heavily on overflights and on monitoring from aircraft, it was spasmodic. Human intelligence is valuable in confirming what may be seen or heard, but it was not easy to find human sources in Cuba.[21] In 1962 the presence of the Soviet missiles was detected primarily by U-2 aircraft overflying the island. That intelligence was supplemented by some voice and human information.

Once that episode was over, the intensity of U.S. intelligence cover of Cuba declined. From 1968 until 1972 there were fragmentary reports suggesting the continued presence in Cuba of Soviet troops.[22] In 1973 and 1974 there were ambiguous reports suggesting artillery exercises by Soviet troops. The first reference to a "brigade" came in 1975. There were further references in 1976 and 1977. In 1978 an intelligence analysis suggested that there had possibly been a Soviet ground force unit in training since 1977.[23]

As noted earlier, growing concern within the administration over Cuban activities in the Caribbean and Central America led National Security Adviser Zbigniew Brzezinski in March of 1979 to order a more intensive review of intelligence on Soviet forces in Cuba. Because of limitations on personnel and other priorities, not all of the communications traffic that had been monitored from Cuba had been fully processed by the National Security Agency.[24] In response to the request from Dr. Brzezinski, analysts in the NSA reviewed previously obtained material. As a result, in mid-July the intelligence analysts reached the conclusion that a brigade existed in Cuba and that it was different in character from the Soviet advisory mission of several thousand personnel working directly with the Cuban armed services.[25]

The fact that the analysts had reached this conclusion was provided to Senator Stone, who had been prodding the intelligence community for reports of Soviet activity in Cuba. So far as is known, he did not, initially, have information on the size or mission of the brigade. When Stone, on July 17, raised the issue in an open hearing with Admirals Moorer and Zumwalt, he asked what their reaction would be if it were discovered that a large group of Soviet combat troops were in Cuba.

In a closed session that afternoon, Stone pressed administration officials on this rumor. Senator Church, the committee chairman, was pressed by Admiral Stansfield Turner, the director of the CIA, to accept the administration's assurances, and Senator Church agreed. He issued a public statement on behalf of the committee, from which only Senator Stone dissented. That statement read:

> In response to a question about the presence of Soviet military personnel in Cuba, Secretary Brown advised the Senate Foreign Relations Committee that there is no evidence of any substantial increase in the size of the Soviet military presence in Cuba over the past several years. Apart from a military group that has been advising the Cuban armed forces for fifteen years or more, our intelligence does not warrant the conclusion that there are any other significant Soviet military forces in Cuba.[26]

On July 24 Senator Stone wrote to President Carter asking the president's comments on reports that there was a Soviet command structure in Cuba. Secretary Vance replied on July 27 on behalf of the president. He used language identical to that in Senator Church's statement and then added, "At the same time the President directed that we give increased attention to the situation and monitor it closely. This is being done. The President raised the question of the Soviet presence in Cuba with President Brezhnev in Vienna and made clear to him that a Soviet buildup would adversely affect our relationship." In the same letter, Secretary Vance referred to the understanding with the Soviets and assured Senator Stone, "We have no evidence that the Soviets are in violation of this understanding."[27]

In addition to the letter, Senator Stone was promised orally that a greater effort would be made to determine if there were other Soviet units on the island. It was clear from conversations with Senator Stone at the time that he was pursuing not only the question of whether a unit existed but, recalling President Carter's letter to him of January 27, 1978, also the question of whether a "base" existed.

In early August, intelligence sources determined that a Soviet training exercise was planned in mid-August on San Pedro beach in Cuba. Alerted to this plan, it was possible to program satellites to photograph the August 17 maneuvers. Not only was the maneuver area photographed but so, also, was the area believed to contain the headquarters of the Soviet brigade. The photographs demonstrated that the units maneuvering on San Pedro beach on August 17 were from the suspected Soviet base, and photographs on subsequent days demonstrated that the equipment had returned to that area. This was considered by the intelligence community to be conclusive proof of the presence of a Soviet armed forces unit. The unit was estimated to have between two thousand and three thousand men equipped with tanks, artillery, and armored personnel carriers. The available intelligence gave no clear proof of the mission of this unit.[28]

The processing of intelligence of this kind and its evaluation can take several days. It was not, therefore, until August 22 that Secretary Vance and other senior officers of the administration were informed of this conclusion. President Carter was informed of the new intelligence during a stop at Hannibal, Missouri, while on a vacation trip on a Mississippi riverboat. Under Secretary of State for Political Affairs David Newsom subsequently telephoned Senator Stone, who was in Florida during a congressional recess, and informed him that the department now had further information on the matter in Cuba in which Senator Stone had demonstrated a strong interest. He promised the senator that he would receive a full briefing on this when the Senate reconvened after Labor Day. Senator Stone expressed satisfaction with this arrangement.

The information on the possible presence of a Soviet brigade in Cuba which had been revealed to Senator Stone in mid-July was made public in an article in the *Washington Star* on July 18 and in broadcasts by Ted Koppel on ABC on July 20 and by John Scali on July 24. None of these stories or broadcasts, however, resulted in any serious attention to the issue, either in the Congress or by the public.

Ironically, it was not the published news stories but the top secret National Intelligence Digest that brought the information to public attention. On August 28, the National Intelligence Digest, which then circulated to some four hundred cleared addressees in the Washington area, carried the results of the intelligence detection of the Cuban unit and referred to it as a "combat" brigade.

There is often a difference of opinion between policymakers and intelligence officers regarding the wisdom of the prompt, wide circulation of information such as this. The policymaker, correctly apprehensive about premature leaks, worries that information of this kind will have an impact before it is fully evaluated. The intelligence officer feels an obligation to clients and is more inclined to move quickly to print.

The result was that on August 29, 1979, Richard Baker, a member of the staff of Under Secretary Newsom, received a telephone call from Clarence Robinson, a staff writer of *Aviation Week* magazine. Robinson said he wished Baker to comment on a piece of information. He then proceeded to read a paragraph which Baker recognized immediately as coming out of the National Intelligence Digest. Baker had been part of a working group contemplating the contingency of a leak of this information and was immediately aware of the significance of the telephone call. He responded that he had no comment, and went immediately to the office of the under secretary.

That telephone call started a process that contributed to setting aside a strategic arms limitation treaty and to further strained relations in general with the Soviet Union. It may even have influenced later Soviet actions, including the invasion of Afghanistan.

FIVE

U.S.-Soviet
Understandings

From the first appearance of the word "brigade" and the recognition of a possible problem with the Congress, Secretary Vance and his advisers were conscious that this would be more a U.S.-Soviet problem than a U.S.-Cuban problem. From the time of the missile crisis in 1962, the United States had considered that the presence of Soviet weapons and Soviet forces in Cuba was a bilateral matter between the Soviets and the United States.

One axiom of diplomacy is, where possible, to avoid surprising other governments with public information that may affect their interests. This applies to friends as well as adversaries. As officials in Washington watched the unfolding of the intelligence on the brigade, they could not exclude the possibility of an early leak. Those who had been involved in previous episodes relating to Soviet systems in Cuba were fully aware that, in other cases, the crisis had begun with a leak of intelligence data.[29] Those who knew the Soviet psychology believed it unlikely that the Soviets would consider a leak of information of this kind inadvertent. Secretary Vance decided to warn them and to give them a chance for an explanation. Clearly he hoped that this might defuse the issue before it became public.

Officials were also aware that when such matters become public, one of the first questions asked by the Congress and the media is: Have you approached the Soviets? They concluded that it was best to be prepared.

Secretary Vance chose for this purpose a channel frequently used to convey less formal messages and to take soundings on sensitive issues with the Soviets. Accordingly, Marshall Shulman, who was on leave as director of the Russian Institute at Columbia University to serve as special assistant for Soviet affairs to Secretary Vance, approached Soviet Minister-Counselor Bessmertnykh on July 27.

In their conversation, Shulman told Bessmertnykh that the United States was closely watching Soviet activities in Cuba. He mentioned that any changes suggesting a heightened offensive capability for the Soviets would evoke serious concern. Conscious of the frequent approaches to the State Department by Senator Stone on buildings at Cienfuegos, Shulman mentioned specifically reports of new facilities at that base. He also referred to the press and television reports of an organized Soviet combat unit in Cuba. Bessmertnykh said that he understood the seriousness of any such development and he would report the conversation to Moscow.

There the matter rested until Richard Baker received the telephone call from *Aviation Week* on the morning of August 29.

Diplomatic encounters between representatives of the United States and the Soviet Union are difficult at best. They are almost always clouded to some degree by deep suspicions and by attitudes growing out of two very different types of systems. Soviet diplomats are accustomed to a rigid centralized authority. They have great difficulty in understanding the diffusion of responsibilities in the U.S. government. They are not sympathetic to the need for public information. In cases involving Cuba, there is also a substantial history, beginning with the 1962 missile crisis.

The discovery of Soviet nuclear missiles in Cuba in October of that year and their subsequent withdrawal by the Soviets under the pressure of U.S. diplomacy represented a watershed in U.S.-Soviet relations. It undoubtedly increased the resistance of the Soviets to any further appearance of retreat from Cuba under U.S. pressure. Not only were Soviet pride and politics involved, so, too, were Soviet relations with Cuba.

While the discussions then and subsequently over Soviet activity in Cuba became exclusively U.S.-Soviet affairs, the Soviet Union could not be indifferent to Cuban reaction.

The missile crisis established certain understandings between the United States and the Soviet Union which, however ambiguous, have become the basis for all further discussions of Soviet weapons systems in Cuba. Questions have arisen three times since 1962 about whether activities of the Soviet Union in Cuba violated the basic understandings reached in 1962. Again, in July 1979, when the word of the brigade was received, analysts in the State Department were asked to look at the understandings.

Understanding the arrangements worked out between the Soviet Union and the United States at the time of the missile crisis is not a simple matter. The understandings actually consist of at least three memoranda of conversations held separately between different representatives of the two countries in New York and in Washington. The generally accepted public statement is contained in an exchange of letters between Chairman Khrushchev and President Kennedy.

On October 26, 1962, Khrushchev had written to Kennedy:

> I propose: we, for our part, will declare that our ships bound for Cuba are not carrying any armaments. You will declare that the United States will not invade Cuba with its troops and will not support any other forces which might intend to invade Cuba.

Included in President Kennedy's response the following day was this language:

> The key elements of our proposal—which seem generally acceptable as I understand them—are as follows: 1) you would agree to remove these weapon systems from Cuba under appropriate United Nations observation and supervision; and undertake, with suitable safeguard, to halt the further introduction of such weapon systems into Cuba. 2) We, on our part, would agree—upon establishment of adequate arrangements through the United Nations—to insure a) to remove promptly the quarantine measures now in effect, and b) to give assurances against any invasion against Cuba.[30]

The exact agreements reached are still the subject of debate. Two unresolved ambiguities remain in this understanding. The first is whether the United States has any commitment, in the absence of a Soviet agreement to remove the missiles under United Nations supervision, to carry out its pledge not to invade Cuba. While this has at times been debated, the removal of Soviet missiles, coupled with a lessened enthusiasm for invading Cuba after the Bay of Pigs episode, has made this ambiguity less significant.[31]

The more significant question which has arisen on three occasions since the original understanding is what types of weapons systems were meant to be excluded and whether the understanding had any application to personnel.[32] The uncertainties have been further clouded by a lack of adequate institutional memory from one administration to another, by imprecise drafting in presidential correspondence, and by pressures generated on issues peripheral to that of weapons systems.

One example of the further ambiguity introduced by subsequent correspondence is the letter mentioned earlier, from President Carter to Senator Stone, in which Carter said, "In particular, it has been and will continue to be the policy of the United States to oppose any efforts, direct or indirect, by the Soviet Union to establish military bases in the Western Hemisphere."[33] The question of "bases" had not been an issue in the 1962 exchanges, although it was raised in 1970 by the Nixon administration. On the basis of that history, Senator Stone sought to make it an issue in 1979 by insisting that the construction of certain buildings at the Cuban naval base at Cienfuegos suggested the establishment of a Soviet base and, hence, was a violation of the original understanding.[34]

*   *   *   *

There was little basis in the original exchanges at the time of the Cuban missile crisis for claiming any understanding on the presence of personnel. The discussion of personnel in 1962 centered solely on those who were servicing and guarding missiles.[35]

The question of the definition of weapons systems to be governed by the understanding of 1962 was first tested in 1970 when an Echo-II class Soviet nuclear-powered submarine, capable of carrying nuclear-powered cruise missiles, stopped at Cienfuegos and Havana. In September 1970, U.S. intelligence detected the deployment of two barges in Cienfuegos. This type of barge had elsewhere been associated with the disposal of effluents from the reactors of nuclear submarines.[36]

A month earlier, Soviet Chargé d'Affaires Yuly M. Vorontsov had called on Henry Kissinger, then the White House national security adviser, and asked for a reaffirmation of the 1962 Kennedy-Khrushchev understanding. Dr. Kissinger, in reply, said: "We defined these as prohibiting the implacement of any offensive weapons or any offensive delivery systems on Cuban territory. We reaffirm that in return we would not use military force to bring about a change in the governmental structure in Cuba." It was clear from this and from subsequent probings, including the deployment of various types of nuclear submarines, that the Soviets were testing the limits of this understanding.[37]

After further study of the submarine deployments, the barges, and some construction on land, the Defense Intelligence Agency concluded in 1970 that these activities "(were) intended to provide the submarines with an increased capability to support the naval operations in the Caribbean area, including those of submarines."[38] The suspicion grew within the Nixon administration that the Soviets were establishing a base for nuclear submarines. No public action was taken; but, in a pattern that was destined to be repeated, on September 24, 1970, Pentagon spokesmen leaked word of the intelligence about Cienfuegos to the press. The next day, at an afternoon press briefing, Dr. Kissinger issued a stern public warning to the Soviets, stating that any establishment of a Soviet base to service missile-firing submarines in Cuba would be regarded as a violation of the 1962 agreement.[39]

The Soviets continued to send both nuclear-powered and nuclear missile submarines to Cuba until November 1974, when nuclear submarine visits to Cuba ended. The submarine episode, while reaffirming that an understanding existed between the United States and the Soviet Union on the deployment of weapons systems, made the nature of the understanding even more ambiguous. The question of what constituted a "base" was never clarified. The question of whether nuclear-powered submarines, submarines with nuclear missiles, or both, violated the understanding was not clear. The term "nuclear sub" was used in statements without an effort to distinguish between propulsion and weapons. Also left unclear was the question of whether the servicing of submarines "in Cuba" or "from Cuba" constituted a violation. Dr. Kissinger had spoken about servicing nuclear submarines in Cuba or from Cuba as being a violation of the understanding. President Nixon, in a statement on January 4, 1971, had further muddied the waters by referring to the servicing of submarines only "from Cuba."[40]

The next event triggering a discussion of the 1962 understandings was the Soviet Union's introduction in April 1978 of MIG-23D aircraft into Cuba. The aircraft were assumed to be part of the Soviet military assistance program to Cuba. The MIG-23 had been provided to other countries but there was one model, the MIG-23D, deployed only in the Soviet Union, with a substantial range and with a capacity to carry nuclear weapons. Their introduction into Cuba once more raised the question of what constituted an offensive weapons system of the kind understood to be covered by the 1962 exchange.

The equipment the Soviet Union had withdrawn from Cuba in 1962 had included Ilyushyn-28 light fighter-bombers. The question arose in 1978 whether the MIG-23D had a nuclear capacity and whether its range made it comparable to the fighter-bombers which were withdrawn in 1962. Once again intelligence was leaked, this time to newspaper columnists Evans and Novak. At least some in the administration suspected that the leak was related to efforts to undermine support for the SALT II Treaty, which was then being negotiated. The issue of Soviet weapons in Cuba and of the 1962 understanding became public once more.[41]

The determination of whether the MIG-23D in question was the Soviet domestic model or an export model required a very precise review of certain features of the aircraft's undercarriage. It was subsequently determined that the aircraft were not nuclear capable and that they were probably considered by the Soviets and the Cubans as an upgrading of older MIG-21 aircraft. The United States was sensitive to creating precedents under which a nation could object to the provision of more modern aircraft to a state receiving military assistance. It was concluded that it was not a violation of the 1962 agreement and that a formal protest was not warranted.

President Carter did enunciate a formula at a televised news conference on November 30, 1978, stating:

We would consider it to be a very serious development if the Soviet Union violated the 1962 agreement. When we have interrogated the Soviet Union through diplomatic channels, they have assured us that no shipments of weapons to the Cubans have or will violate the terms of the 1962 agreement. We will monitor their compliance with this agreement very carefully, which we have been doing in the past, both as to the quality of weapons sent there and the quantity of weapons sent there, to be sure that there is no offensive threat to the United States possible from Cuba.[42]

Clearly the Soviet brigade in Cuba did not constitute an offensive threat comparable to ballistic missiles, nuclear submarines, or modern fighter-bomber aircraft. The experience of those three episodes, however, was in the minds of those dealing with the brigade issue.

They noted that, in each case, the Soviets had taken seriously the U.S. approach. The Soviets had reaffirmed that an understanding existed. They had responded, without public commitment, by limiting their deployment and activities. Undoubtedly the Carter administration hoped that, if the Soviets were approached in a similar vein on the brigade, the pattern would repeat itself.

S I X

Informing Congress
and the Soviets

Two domestic institutions, the Congress and the media, are significant actors in nearly every major U.S. foreign policy crisis. Leaks to the media, while they may not create a crisis, can accelerate the pace at which decisions are made. Congressional interest similarly pushes the process of decisions. Even if Congress is not initially involved, the policymaker must ensure that Congress is not left out.

In the case of the Soviet brigade in Cuba, a senator's interest was one element pushing an administration to gather further intelligence on Cuba. The media's possession of that intelligence sparked actions which magnified the issues.

When Richard Baker came into the office of Under Secretary Newsom on that Wednesday morning and announced that *Aviation Week* had the item from the National Intelligence Digest, the under secretary's immediate thought was of two elements in the situation, the Soviets and the Congress. Already the Soviets had a hint of the problem in the conversation between Dr. Shulman and Mr. Bessmertnykh. Senator Stone knew, from the earlier telephone call from the under secretary, that the State Department had additional intelligence. He did not yet have the details. No other members of Congress had as yet been advised.

Newsom, upon hearing Baker's information, buzzed the office of the secretary and in a few minutes had apprised Secretary Vance of the latest developments. Although *Aviation Week* would not appear before Congress reconvened on September 5, the officials could not assume that the information would hold until that day. Magazines such as *Aviation Week* were known to give such information to daily newspapers or to the television networks in advance of their own publication. If *Aviation Week* had the story, others might have it too. The item could be published at any time.

Secretary Vance's primary concern was the impact on the SALT agreement, already encountering heavy weather in Congress. His first thought was to reach the Soviets. Given their interest in SALT, he hoped they would find common cause and make such adjustments as necessary to minimize the issue. His second concern was to ensure that key members of Congress knew of and saw the matter in perspective before they read about it in the press.

One member of Congress had taken the initiative on the issue. That did not relieve the State Department, if proper relations with Congress were to be maintained, of a responsibility to inform the chairman of the Senate Foreign Relations Committee and other key members of both houses. Senator Stone, who had already been informed, was a member of the committee. A chairman who reads in the press information that has already been given on a private basis to one member feels that his own prerogatives are being ignored. As chairman, Senator Church was very important to the administration, particularly in guiding the SALT treaty through the Senate.

The end of August, in the midst of the Labor Day congressional recess, is a time of maximum dispersal in Washington. That fall in 1979 was no exception. Soviet Ambassador Anatoly Dobrynin, with whom Mr. Vance and his predecessors had frequently worked out many difficult problems, was in Moscow, where his father and mother were seriously ill. The department had no indication of when he might return. President Carter was on a boat on the Mississippi, Vice President Mondale was in China, the national security adviser, Dr. Brzezinski, was on vacation, and senators and congressmen were either campaigning or traveling abroad.

The secretary gathered together his key advisers, including Under Secretary Newsom, Marshall Shulman, Robert Berry of the Bureau of European Affairs, Peter Tarnoff, the head of the executive secretariat, and Hodding Carter, the press spokesman. The concerns on the minds of the secretary and his advisers in this meeting were how to deal, first, with the Soviets, second, with the members of Congress, and third, with the press. There was a discussion of points of leverage the United States might have on Cuba in encouraging Cuba to remove the Soviet forces. A request was made to examine the possible applicability to the brigade situation of the Monroe Doctrine, the Rio Treaty, and the charter of the Organization of American States. It was subsequently concluded that a strong basis for mobilizing international support for the departure of the brigade did not exist in any of these instruments.[43]

The group decided it was important to have one agreed position on the brigade which could be used not only for the discussions with the Soviets but for the briefing of members of Congress and the press as necessary. A statement, therefore, was prepared. The statement, as drafted, was as follows:

> We have recently confirmed the presence in Cuba of what appears to be a Soviet combat unit. This is the first time we have been able to confirm the presence of a Soviet ground forces unit on the island.
>
> Elements of the unit appear to have been there since at least 1976. We estimate that it consists of some two thousand to three thousand men. The unit includes armored, artillery and infantry elements. In addition, we estimate that the Soviet Union maintains between 1,500 and 2,000 military advisory and technical personnel in Cuba.
>
> As currently configured and supported the unit poses no threat to the United States.
>
> Ground forces *per se* did not figure in our bilateral understandings with the Soviets which were directed toward offensive weapons systems.
>
> Nonetheless we are concerned about the presence of Soviet combat troops in Cuba.
>
> We have in recent months raised with the Soviets the issue of the Soviet-Cuban military relationship. On August 29 we called in the Soviet Chargé

to express our concerns about this Soviet ground force unit. We will continue our discussions with them on this subject.

We will of course continue to monitor all aspects of Soviet military activities in Cuba to ensure there is no threat to the United States.[44]

In the absence of Ambassador Dobrynin, it was decided that Under Secretary Newsom would see Vladillian Vasev, the chargé d'affaires of the Soviet Union, that afternoon and that Newsom, on the following day (Thursday), would telephone key members of Congress.

The meeting between Newsom and Vasev was brief and formal. Newsom had been instructed to mention information the U.S. government had received that a brigade equipped with combat weapons was present in Cuba. Because of the importance of Soviet-American relationships and a continued understanding between the two countries, the State Department wished to inform the Soviet embassy and to seek an explanation of the presence of this unit in Cuba. Newsom was also to pass the message that Secretary Vance hoped to see Ambassador Dobrynin as soon as possible after his return to Washington.

Newsom delivered the message to Vasev. Vasev's immediate response was to ask on what legal basis was the United States raising the issue. He was clearly referring to the 1962 understandings. Newsom replied that the question was being raised because of the importance of a good understanding between the two countries, particularly at a time when an important treaty was before the Senate. Vasev again asked whether the United States had any basis for questioning the presence of Soviet troops in Cuba. He emphasized that this was a matter primarily between Cuba and the Soviet Union.

Newsom stressed that the revelation of this new dimension of Soviet presence in Cuba would undoubtedly cause concern in the United States, particularly in the Congress. He hoped that the Soviet Union might provide an explanation that would assist the administration in dealing with the expected inquiry. Vasev, unmoved, informed Newsom that he would report the conversation to Moscow and that he would seek to provide the department information on when Ambassador Dobrynin might return.[45]

The next day Under Secretary Newsom telephoned key members of

Congress, including the majority and minority leaders in the Senate, and the chairmen and ranking minority members of the Senate Foreign Relations Committee and the House Foreign Affairs Committee.

Senator Javits, the ranking Republican member of the Foreign Relations Committee, was in New York. He took the presentation calmly and expressed the hope that the matter would not be blown out of proportion.

The reaction of Senators Robert Byrd and Howard Baker, majority and minority leaders of the Senate, was similar. Chairman Clement Zablocki and members of his House Foreign Affairs Committee were traveling in Europe. Newsom reached them in Brussels. Zablocki asked that Newsom dictate the statement from which he was reading to a staff member so that it could be circulated to members of the committee. He had no further comment.

Newsom again reached Senator Stone in Florida and gave him further information on the nature of the intelligence. He informed him that there was the possibility that it would become public. Senator Stone did not react immediately. The next day he gave a press conference, probably sparked by that which Senator Church had given the day before.

Senator Church, the chairman of the committee, was campaigning in Idaho. Newsom reached him from his home late that evening. He reacted sharply to the information. His first words were, "That will sink SALT." He asked whether the department intended to release this information and was told that that was not the intention. The under secretary emphasized that the brigade posed no threat to the United States, and that efforts were being made to seek further information.

Senator Church subsequently telephoned Secretary Vance and informed the secretary of his feeling that, if no one else was going to make it public, he should do so. The secretary replied, "We'll trust you to use your judgment on that, Senator," but urged the chairman not to blow the affair out of proportion. He again emphasized that the State Department was seeking negotiations with the Soviets to avoid a serious crisis. The senator, after an unsuccessful effort to reach the president, called a press conference that evening, disclosed the information he had received, and urged that the Soviets remove the troops from Cuba.[46]

The State Department did not comment on Senator Church's statement until the regular noon briefing for reporters on Friday, August 31. Hodding Carter read the statement that had formed the basis for the briefing and took an extensive series of questions. The questioning covered some twenty pages of transcript.[47]

Questions and comments by the press focused on whether the presence of these troops constituted a "base," what their purpose was, and why the administration had not immediately called for them to be removed. Several questions dealt with the possible link betweeen the presence and removal of these troops and the ratification of SALT. One questioner raised the earlier statements made to Senator Stone that there was no evidence of any substantial increase of Soviet military presence in Cuba over the last several years and asked why the administration had changed its views in so short a time. There were further questions about the possibility of additional surveillance of Cuba. Hodding Carter turned away all questions relating to intelligence methods.

One questioner asked whether there was any evidence of an airlift capacity or a sea transport capacity available to these troops. Hodding Carter "took the question," meaning that he would seek to get an answer. That answer was to figure in the administration's later response to the issue. He similarly dodged efforts to obtain a commitment on a demand for the removal of the troops.

At one point in the briefing Hodding Carter, increasingly exasperated by the nature of some of the questions, said the following:

> Wait a minute. If you're asking me to repeat myself about the concern we feel about what is a serious situation, then I will repeat that concern and tell you that we are raising it because we view it as a serious matter; but I'm not really going to speculate with you as to what we might do.
>
> I was rereading the transcript on the Kennedy thing, as a matter of fact, and one of the interesting aspects of it that I would remind all of you is that for eleven days you were shut out entirely and there was a great deal of complaint about the operation of both Mr. Sylvester and Mr. Manning, who had my job then, in making sure you weren't informed as this thing progressed.
>
> The reason the President gave in his press conference for not doing it was precisely not to deal with questions such as you are asking me right now while he was in the middle of the diplomatic negotiations. We are in

the middle of a diplomatic negotiation. A lot of this, we are just simply not going to be able to deal with.[48]

The stage was clearly set for an escalating confrontation with the press, with the Congress, and with the Soviets over a Soviet brigade in Cuba.

Managing the Issue

The diplomacy of the United States, on any major issue, is likely to include formal negotiations with a foreign government, separate—and sometimes conflicting—expressions from within the U.S. government, and more than one channel of communication. Efforts to reach agreement with another country occur also against the backdrop of press questions, congressional curiosity, and public reaction. The foreign government that is a sophisticated observer of the United States will look to each of these elements for clues as to the real strengths and intentions of the U.S. government. All of these elements were present in the effort to resolve the issue of the Soviet brigade in Cuba.

The responsibility for the conduct of the formal negotiations lay with the secretary of state. By tradition, the Department of State has the responsibility for diplomatic negotiations. It does not always follow, in reality, that this is the case. Presidents, presidential observers, cabinet officers, and even self- or presidentially appointed special envoys have served this role.[49] In the case of the Soviet brigade, Secretary Vance had the primary responsibility for the strategy of negotiating the SALT treaty and conducting its passage through the Senate, even though he had at times been required to share direct contacts with the Soviet Union with others, including Dr. Brzezinski. When the brigade issue arose, Secretary Vance was the most senior official in Washington. He naturally assumed a direct role in the strategy of response.

Though the secretary of state may conduct the discussions with foreign representatives, the position he takes in international negotiations is almost always the product of consultations within the U.S. executive and, at times, with the leadership of the Congress. The president, key presidential advisers, and other cabinet officers share in the decisions. The secretary of state, whatever his personal style, is expected to represent this wider consensus. Those with other views are likely to remind the secretary of their points of view by public statements during the course of the negotiations.

In the brigade issue, Secretary Vance saw as his first task to buy time until he could talk directly with Ambassador Anatoly Dobrynin. His longer-range hope was that he could work out a solution with Dobrynin that would save SALT II in the Senate and restore some degree of stability to relations with the Soviet Union. He was conscious that Foreign Minister Gromyko would be making his annual visit to the United Nations General Assembly at the end of September.

In approaching the talks with Dobrynin, Secretary Vance also desired a minimum of public discussion of the approach to the talks and of the substance of the U.S. position. For a brief time over the Labor Day weekend it looked as if the secretary might have the benefit of diminished public interest. Media attention was mild. While there were references to the brigade on the television networks, the Sunday edition of the *New York Times* of September 3 did not mention the issue.

The secretary, nevertheless, concluded that, with the return of Congress after the recess, a higher-level statement than that issued by Hodding Carter on August 31 was needed. He decided to hold a press conference on September 5, the day Congress reconvened. His objectives were to defuse the issue, if possible, to put the matter in some perspective, and to report his plans to discuss the issue with the Soviet ambassador. His statement was also designed to set the stage for the substance of his discussions with the Soviets.

On the basis of talks with his advisers, he concluded that it would be difficult to get the Soviets to withdraw the unit or to add any formal supplemental agreements to the understandings on weapons systems reached in 1962 and reaffirmed in 1970. The Soviets remained determined that there would be no more withdrawals of the type Khrushchev agreed to in 1962.

In framing the position for his statement, the secretary was also proceeding without any clearer idea of the function of the unit than that presented by the photographic and electronic intelligence. He judged his best tactic lay in an ambiguous and flexible approach. If, as he suspected, the Soviets were not prepared to withdraw the unit, but were interested in saving SALT, he wanted the way open to alter the function or composition of the brigade to fit the political need. It was on this basis that he devised the statement that the United States "would not be satisfied with the status quo." He believed that this relatively vague formula would provide an opportunity for diplomatic maneuver. He received the president's approval to this approach.[50]

In his opening statement at the press conference of September 5, Secretary Vance stressed that this was a "serious matter," and, without specifically mentioning the Monroe Doctrine, said that "the presence of the unit runs counter to long-held American policies." The Doctrine itself was not mentioned, because of a lack of consensus within the administration as to its applicability to this situation.

Repeating the data gained from the intelligence, Vance acknowledged that the mission of the unit was "unclear," that it had no "assault capability," and that it was not covered by existing bilateral understandings. He announced that he would be "pursuing this matter with the Soviets in the coming days." As planned, he responded to the first question about a possible request to the Soviets to remove the troops by saying, "Let me say very simply that I will not be satisfied with the maintenance of the status quo."[51]

He testified along similar lines the same day before the Senate Foreign Relations Committee.

The brigade issue was less of a media issue than it was a political issue. Because the momentum was in the Congress, the secretary's press conference and his appearance before the Senate Foreign Relations Committee did not have the hoped-for effect of buying time until he could negotiate the matter with the Soviet ambassador.

The Republicans, particularly former President Ford and former Secretary of State Kissinger, were offended at the suggestion that the brigade had been in Cuba for "some time." They saw that reference as an effort to throw responsibility onto the previous administration.[52]

The opponents of SALT and those who had been uncomfortable in supporting the SALT agreement saw an opportunity to build further fire against that treaty. Senator Church called for a postponement of the SALT debate scheduled to begin after Labor Day.[53] Although Senator Jacob Javits, ranking Republican member of the Foreign Relations Committee, made an effort to play down the significance of the brigade, other senators saw opportunities to press their own political views. Democratic Senator Henry Jackson, a firm opponent of SALT, cited the Monroe Doctrine. He urged that all Soviet aircraft be removed and that there be no more Soviet submarines in Cuba. He criticized Carter for cancelling the SR-71 intelligence flights over Cuba.[54]

In the absence of any hard information, others speculated on the possible role of such a brigade. Some suggested that it was there to train the Cubans who were deployed to Africa, others that it was a Soviet "tripwire," and still others that it was a Praetorian guard for Castro. It was clear that the combined voices of the Senate were moving in the direction of requiring withdrawal of the brigade as a price for SALT II ratification.

The dimensions of the issue became still clearer when, in the afternoon of September 5, Soviet Chargé Vasev delivered to Deputy Secretary Warren Christopher the Soviet government's response to the request for clarification made by Under Secretary Newsom to Vasev on August 29. The Soviet reply, substantially published in *Pravda* on September 10, said that there had existed for seventeen years a training center in Cuba where Soviet military specialists train Cuban officers in the use and maintenance of Soviet military equipment in the inventory of the Cuban armed forces.[55]

Although President Carter had approved the statement made by Secretary Vance on September 5, the president had not yet been publicly involved in the issue. At a White House policy breakfast on September 7, those gathered decided that the president should make a televised address that evening.[56]

The question of presidential involvement is always one of the more difficult elements in crisis management. Part, of course, will depend upon the president's own personality and desire to be involved. To the extent his advisers are consulted, they must consider whether the problem is manageable, so that the president is not identified with an issue that has no resolution. They must decide whether the involvement of the president will, perhaps, elevate the question to higher levels in other governments, either advancing or, in some cases, frustrating a solution. Presidential involvement sometimes also has the tendency to alarm by giving an issue greater significance than it may actually have. All of these considerations were reviewed. It was decided, however, that the issue had become of sufficient significance for presidential involvement and that both the future of SALT and the credibility of the president's own leadership were involved.

The preparation of a presidential statement inevitably involves the reconciliation of different objectives and points of view within an administration. In this case Secretary Vance and the experts in the State Department desired to focus attention specifically on the presence of the brigade, to leave the way open as much as possible for some form of Soviet accommodation through diplomacy, and to discourage discourse on general Soviet behavior. The president's immediate White House advisers, on the other hand, were sensitive to what they believed to be the president's political vulnerability to charges that he was soft on the Soviets. They wanted to use the presence of the brigade as an example of general Soviet and Cuban aggressive acts and insensitivity to the interests of the United States.

Two statements in the president's TV speech of September 7 represented the emphasis desired by these advisers:

> We are confident about our ability to defend our country or any of our friends from external aggression. The issue posed is of a different nature. It involves the stationing of Soviet combat troops here in the Western Hemisphere, in a country which acts as a Soviet proxy in military adventures in other areas of the world like Africa.

We do have the right to insist that the Soviet Union respect our interests and our concerns if the Soviet Union expects us to respect their sensibilities and their concerns. Otherwise, relations between our two countries will inevitably be adversely affected.[57]

The president's speech did, however, follow the basic strategy, calling for "calm" and a "sense of proportion" and emphasizing that this was a time for "firm diplomacy."

In a separate interview with the *Washington Post* on the day of the president's speech, Dr. Brzezinski spelled out his views more explicitly, referring to Cuba's nonalignment as "fundamentally ridiculous" and calling Castro a "puppet," totally dependent on the Soviet Union, "a surrogate," and a "dependent client."[58]

On September 9, Soviet Ambassador Dobrynin returned to Washington. He and Secretary Vance met on September 10. Together there were eight U.S.-Soviet meetings, six between Secretary Vance and Ambassador Dobrynin and two between Vance and Foreign Minister Gromyko. There was one exchange between President Carter and Chairman Brezhnev. In addition, Senate Majority Leader Byrd had a secret meeting with Dobrynin.[59]

The secretary's task was to convey to Ambassador Dobrynin a sense of the political problem created in the United States by the discovery of a brigade of Soviet troops equipped with forty tanks, sixty armored personnel carriers, and various other pieces of hardware. The ambassador, who had been in Washington for more than twenty years, including the period of the 1962 Cuban missile crisis, presumably understood the sensitivities and currents in the American political system. As a member of the Central Committee of the Soviet Communist Party, he was presumed, also, to have both considerable access and influence in Moscow. It was not at all clear, however, that he was able to convey some of the unpredictable twists and turns of the Washington scene in a comprehensible fashion to Moscow or whether, if he did try, those who were making the decisions in Moscow could fully understand.[60]

The Dobrynin channel had been used frequently by previous secretaries of state. The U.S. embassy in Moscow was used much less on significant issues because of a feeling in Washington that Dobrynin's messages would pass through fewer hands in Moscow and would benefit from Dobrynin's own reporting of the background and atmosphere. The U.S. embassy in Moscow, during the Soviet brigade crisis, was kept generally informed, but was not sent precise information on each meeting. U.S. Ambassador to the Soviet Union Malcolm Toon objected strongly to this arrangement. He believed that at the least a parallel approach would serve to reinforce and check what Dobrynin was sending.

Secretary Vance usually saw Dobrynin alone, although on occasions they were joined by Marshall Shulman. A paper of "talking points" was customarily prepared and reviewed with the White House staff and, at times, the president himself. On some occasions, to reinforce his approach, the secretary would give the "talking points" to Dobrynin. In diplomacy such "non-papers" serve the purpose of ensuring the accuracy of understanding without being seen as formal documents.

In the initial talks on the brigade, Secretary Vance sought to obtain more information on the unit and to test the Soviet desire to resolve the problem and the degree of Soviet flexibility in responding to the U.S. concerns. He faced a number of problems.

Clearly, the most desirable outcome from the administration's standpoint was the withdrawal of the unit. There was little indication that the Soviets would agree to this. The *Pravda* editorial, published and circulated through TASS on the day of the first Vance-Dobrynin meeting, referred to a "training center" that had not changed its function since 1962. Saying that the Soviet personnel were there at Cuba's request solely to aid that country's defense, *Pravda* declared that "any attempts to restrict the right (of defense) are in crying contradiction with accepted norms of international intercourse and are absolutely unfounded." The editorial focused on members of Congress for "alarm-spreading statements" and asserted that "it is not by chance that all this outcry is being used by circles in the U.S. that are trying to prevent ratification of the SALT II treaty and, in any case, to complicate its ratification." The editorial also suggested it was an American ploy to embarrass Cuba on the eve of the nonaligned nations' conference which opened September 3 in Havana.[61] The editorial gave little hope that Dobrynin would have the flexibility to move far away from the public Soviet position.

The secretary's task was complicated, also, by the use of the word "combat." Because of the associated equipment and organization, the original intelligence note which leaked to Senator Stone and *Aviation Week* referred to a "Soviet combat brigade." Words such as "combat" in classified documents readily catch the eye of someone looking for startling information. As the *Washington Post* noted in its review of the brigade issue on October 16, 1979:

> The word, combat, had not been used in the findings before but there is no indication that its threatening connotations and political implications were appreciated, or even examined, at the time.
> Intelligence officials later explained that the "Soviet combat brigade" was so described to distinguish it from a training outfit. Once the words had been repeated in internal documents, with wide circulation and even public statements, "we can't back off," an inquiring official was told.[62]

The use of the term "combat" also made it difficult for the United States to accept the Soviet position that the unit as equipped was there for training. Some conspicuous change in the equipment and formation of the unit would be necessary, in Washington's eyes, if the term "training" was to be credible. Only with demonstrable changes would the change in the "status quo" become credible in the eyes of the public.

The political sensitivity of this aspect was demonstrated when on September 12 Under Secretary Newsom met at lunch with a group of reporters. In the course of the informal conversation, Newsom mentioned several possible purposes of the unit, making it clear that no one yet knew its exact purpose. One speculative possibility was that it was there to assist Cubans in "unit" exercise training. Reporters picked this up as a "trial balloon" and it was given front page treatment in both the *Washington Post* and the *New York Times*.[63] The reporters suggested that the administration was considering this as one approach that could reconcile the equipment of the unit and the Soviet contention that it was a "training center."

The stories brought strong denials from both the White House and the State Department, but not before some senators had denounced the idea on suspicion that the State Department was seeking to "rationalize" the presence of the brigade. Senator Jackson remarked, "This will go over like a lead balloon.'' He insisted that the unit was part of a Soviet plan to build "Fortress Cuba." He repeated his insistence that the unit be withdrawn.[64]

The first four meetings with Dobrynin were exploratory. The secretary expressed the U.S. concern over the unit and U.S. sensitivity about what happens in Cuba, and sought further information on the unit. Dobrynin reported each conversation to Moscow, but continued throughout to insist that the unit was associated with the training of Cuban forces and had been in its present location for seventeen years.

By the end of the fourth meeting, it was clear that there was little "give" in the Soviet position. On September 17, members of the Policy Review Committee, the president's senior advisers, met under Secretary Vance's chairmanship. They considered specific proposals to deal with both the immediate discussions with the Soviets and the contingency that these talks and subsequent talks with Foreign Minister Gromyko might remain at an impasse.[65]

On September 20, Secretary Vance placed before Dobrynin specific proposals growing out of that meeting to pave the way for discussions with Foreign Minister Gromyko in New York on September 22. These proposals included dissolution of the brigade, reassignment of personnel to advisory duty, and the distribution of the unit's tanks and artillery to the Cubans.[66]

The public background to the talks continued. Soviet media highlighted statements by American politicians such as George McGovern, who was on record urging that the brigade issue not jeopardize SALT ratification. Soviet commentators stressed the presence of U.S. forces in Guantánamo, Turkey, and Norway. They continued to blame the creation of the issue on the enemies of SALT.

Speeches of both Secretary Vance and Foreign Minister Gromyko before the United Nations General Assembly on September 24 and 25 indirectly referred to the brigade issue. Gromyko charged that "all sorts of falsehoods are being piled up concerning the policies of Cuba and the Soviet Union." Without saying to whom the admonition was addressed, he stated, "Our advice on this score is simple: It is high time you honestly admit this whole affair is artificial and is proclaimed to be closed.'' Vance, in his speech the day before, referred to the argument over the brigade as part of a "mixed pattern of U.S.-Soviet relations in an era of far-reaching change.''

Secretary Vance met twice privately with Gromyko in New York, once on September 22 and once on September 27. The two lengthy meetings produced no results. Gromyko persisted in the Soviet position that the crisis was artificially created, that the Soviet force was not a combat unit and was nothing new, and that its presence did not violate any U.S.-Soviet understandings regarding Cuba or threaten the security of the United States.[67]

As the president prepared to meet once more with his senior advisers, there were further public indications of the type of debate going on within the U.S. government.

On September 23, Bernard Gwertzman in the *New York Times* reported Zbigniew Brzezinski's belief that the "Soviet combat brigade in Cuba stems from a Soviet 'pattern of disregard' for American interests" and his warning "of possible retaliation if the Russians failed to co-operate in finding a solution." Brzezinski expressed again his view that " 'the brigade is present in a country which itself is using force around the world to promote its own ideological aspirations and uses that force occasionally, directly or indirectly, against our interests.' " Gwertzman commented:

> Mr. Brzezinski's tone and approach underscored the continuing differences of approach within the Administration. He regards the Soviet brigade as part of a larger problem of Soviet aggressive activity around the world, insensitive to American interests. The State Department tends to look at issues in greater isolation and to see the brigade question in less universal terms.[68]

The next day, on September 24, the Evans and Novak column in the *Washington Post* queried, "Hard or Soft on Cuba?" Speaking of President Carter, the column said, "Nobody knows whether he will follow national security adviser Zbigniew Brzezinski's advice and order a balanced buildup of U.S. power in response to Moscow's intransigence or whether he will maneuver out of the crisis with a face-saving gesture, as the State Department would prefer.''[69]

The measures proposed at the September 17 policy meeting and considered further at a resumed meeting September 27 were of three types. One set, relating to Cuba, would include a resumption of SR-71 flights and an increase in U.S. troop strength at Guantánamo and in the Caribbean. A second set involved economic and political penalties against the Soviet Union, such as reduced sales of high technology, and continued denial of most-favored-nation treatment. A third, even more controversial for Moscow, might include arms sales to China.[70]

At meetings of the Policy Review Committee on September 27 and 28, the decision was taken that President Carter would address the nation; in that address, he would announce selected actions from these proposals. The president decided, at the same time, to consult a group of prominent Americans, including former secretaries of state.[71] On the basis of their advice, the meetings of the Policy Review Committee, and the results of the Vance-Gromyko meetings, it was decided that the president would make a major television statement, hoping, thereby, to lay the matter to rest. The "status quo" would be changed by unilateral U.S. actions. President Carter supplemented the Vance meetings with Gromyko and Dobrynin by a direct "hot line" exchange with Brezhnev that yielded little more than Secretary Vance had been able to secure.

The president's speech of October 1 was a major presentation preceded by letters to other world leaders, congressional briefings, backgrounder meetings with the press, and a pre-speech brief for the diplomatic corps in Washington. A ten-page background paper with questions and answers on the issue[72] was also distributed in advance of the speech.

President Carter's October 1 speech was primarily an effort, almost a final effort, to save SALT II. He repeated what previous statements had said: that the brigade was not a threat but that it represented a challenge to U.S. determination to respond effectively to Soviet competition and to Cuban military activities around the world. He mentioned that some forces had stayed behind in Cuba after the withdrawal of the missiles in 1962 and that there was evidence that some of these forces "had been organized into a combat unit." He suggested that that unit had existed perhaps since the mid-1970s and possibly even longer. He called the brigade "a manifestation of Moscow's dominance of Cuba."

In reference to the only specific result of the extended discussions with the Soviets on the issue, the president detailed a series of points, which he referred to first as "statements" and then as "assurances" from the Soviets.

How the president was to refer to the series of points that came out of the discussions with the Soviets had been a matter of considerable debate during the preparation of the president's speech. The only outcome of the secretary's discussions with the Soviets had been a reiteration that this unit was not a combat unit and that it represented nothing new, and a reaffirmation of the U.S.-Soviet understandings. The president's advisers, who wished to put a positive gloss on the results of the diplomacy, suggested that these be pictured as assurances from the Soviets. Others who were less confident in the word of the Soviets and in the credibility of this approach suggested that they be called only statements. The president actually compromised between these two positions in the following language in his speech:

> The Soviet Union does not admit that the unit in question is a combat unit. However, the Soviets have made certain statements to us with respect to our concern:
>
> — That the unit in question is a training center, that it does nothing more than training, and can do nothing more;
>
> — That they will not change its function or status as a training center. We understand this to mean that they do not intend to enlarge the unit or to give it additional capabilities;
>
> — They have said that the Soviet personnel in Cuba are not and will not be a threat to the United States or to any other nation;
>
> — That they reaffirm the 1962 understanding and the mutually agreed upon confirmation in 1970 and will abide by it in the future. We for our part, reconfirm this understanding.[73]

"These assurances have been given to me," he added, "from the highest level of the Soviet government," referring to his exchange with Brezhnev.

President Carter then outlined a number of steps the United States would take, including increased surveillance of Cuba; the establishment of a military joint task force headquarters at Key West, Florida; expanded military maneuvers; an increase in economic assistance to the Caribbean region; and a directive to the secretary of defense to enhance the capacity of a rapid deployment force. He mentioned the U.S. naval presence in the Indian Ocean and reported that the United States was enhancing its intelligence capability in order to monitor both Soviet and Cuban military activities. He concluded his speech with a strong plea for the ratification of the SALT II agreement.

It was clear from the speech that the advocates of some of the stronger actions did not prevail in the policy discussions. The suspicion remained, however, that decisions had been made on a "hidden agenda" of actions similar to those Dr. Brzezinski had mentioned in his interview of September 22.[74] Shortly after the president's speech the word leaked out that the secretary of defense, Harold Brown, would be making a visit to the People's Republic of China.[75]

The speech did not end the debate. Many, including Senator Stone, called the responses inadequate.[76] The discussion of the brigade issue continued through October. In the middle of October McGeorge Bundy, national security adviser in the Kennedy administration, publicly revealed that the administration had agreed in 1963 that a Soviet brigade at exactly the same location could remain in Cuba. Past testimony given by then Secretary of Defense Robert McNamara to the Senate Armed Services Committee supported Bundy's statement. The Soviets had been correct.[77]

On October 2 the Senate, unmoved by the administration's efforts, adopted a resolution saying that SALT could not be ratified until the president had assured the Senate that Soviet troops in Cuba were not engaged in a combat role.

On December 25 the Soviet Union invaded Afghanistan. Any possibility of recovering SALT ratification from the negative effects of the brigade issue ended with that invasion.

EIGHT

Conclusion

The bizarre episode of the Soviet brigade in Cuba had an impact out of all proportion to the circumstances. It seems clear that the unit that created the uproar was the successor to the one present in 1962, which had remained with at least the tacit consent of the Kennedy administration. It was equally clear that this unit of less than three thousand men, without any apparent assigned or immediately available sea transport or airlift, posed no military threat to the United States; there was certainly no basis for comparison with the missiles of 1962, the submarines of 1970, or the MIG-23s of 1978.

There were those in the administration who suggested during the crisis period of September and October that the brigade was the successor of similar units that stayed in Cuba after 1962. That view was not accepted, in part because some believed that dismissing the brigade on that basis would not have been credible to those who raised the issue. Some may have preferred to let the matter run, believing that it emphasized the lack of Soviet attention to American sensitivities. Whatever the political motives, the affair also demonstrated an acute lack of easy capacity within the United States government to "recall" information, particularly when such information may be in a Defense Department channel and the newer crisis is being handled by the State Department.

The "disclosure" dealt a near-fatal blow to a strategic arms limitation treaty already in trouble. Though the verification of missile launchings required for SALT is a very different matter from finding and identifying a small unit in Cuba, opponents of the treaty used this to demonstrate the difficulty of verifying the SALT treaty. Those already suspicious of Soviet motives and doubtful of Soviet willingness to abide by treaty terms ignored the unit's history and assumed that the Soviets had only recently inserted this brigade. The loss of at least one key supporter of SALT, Senator Russell Long of Louisiana, was directly attributable to the brigade affair.[78] Senator Church used the episode to suggest postponement of hearings. Senator Jackson used it for stepped up attacks on SALT and the administration. The *Washington Post* reported on September 27:

> The only SALT consensus discernible today is that the treaty is in political trouble. When the first month of Senate hearings ended in early August, there were signs of an emerging agreement among a strong majority that SALT was a small but useful step, provided it was accompanied by rigorous defense programs and a firm foreign policy. If that notion now collapses along with the treaty, there is no evidence of a successor consensus that could take its place.[79]

The administration sought to regain the initiative. No one will ever know whether, without Afghanistan, the badly scarred treaty might have recovered.

Only if one were able to look into the secret workings of the Soviet Politburo would it be possible to assess the full effect of this episode, not only on relations with the United States, but on broader Soviet policy. The Soviet leadership were obviously puzzled by the event. They could not believe that the United States, with its sophisticated intelligence, could not have known of the presence of the unit through all the years of its existence. They could not believe that the information retrieval capacity of the United States was so poor that the fact of a similar unit having been the subject of discussion in 1962 would not immediately have come to light. They could only surmise, as they did, that there was a motive for the creation of what they insisted throughout was an "artificial issue."

Members of the Soviet embassy in Washington believed—and probably reported to Moscow—that this was a means chosen by some in the Carter administration to provide a way out for SALT when it appeared that Senate ratification was unlikely. What the Soviets apparently did conclude was that the price demanded—the withdrawal of the unit— was too great for them to pay for the ratification of the SALT treaty in which Brezhnev had invested so much effort. This conclusion was probably reinforced by their growing doubt that the treaty could ever be ratified.

Did this mean that, in late November 1979, when the Politburo was making the final decisions about Soviet policies in Afghanistan, they concluded that relations with the United States were already so bad and the fate of SALT so clearly sealed that concern over provoking the United States need no longer be a deterrent to actions they considered to be in their interest? Or, did they believe, having perceived a weak and confused response to the brigade issue, that there was little the United States could do in reaction to an invasion of Afghanistan?

If the brigade issue meant that the Soviets were now less attentive to the concerns of the United States, then it meant also a strengthened hand of those in the United States deeply suspicious of the Soviets. Such persons were not prepared to accept the validity of the assurances repeated by President Carter in his October 1 speech. The lack of a clear explanation by the Soviets of the purposes of the unit left the way open for continuing rumors and speculation about Soviet activities in Cuba.[80]

America's allies in Europe also found the episode disturbing. To them it was another manifestation of the curious and unpredictable nature of U.S. politics. It reawakened their fears about the steadfastness of U.S. interest in arms control and U.S. tendencies to provoke the Soviet Union. Europeans saw more clearly than many in the United States the disproportionality of the response to the circumstance. Not even these other democracies could fully grasp the manner in which such a crisis could develop out of the strange dynamics of the American democracy.

If Europeans could not understand the nature of American politics and opinion, the incredulity was even greater in the Third World. The suspicion that the brigade was "discovered" to embarrass the non-aligned nations conference that opened in Havana on September 3 was not confined to Cuba and the radicals. The possibility that this suspicion may have lessened the determination of the moderate countries to oppose Castro and the radicals would be hard to document. Tito opposed certain of Castro's measures at Havana for his own sake, not for the sake of the United States. In any event, after the brigade was discovered, there was insufficient support for the United States at Havana to prevent the passage of a resolution calling for the elimination of all U.S. bases around the world.

Some in the administration hoped that the revelation during the non-aligned nations conference of the presence of a Soviet unit in Havana would serve to strengthen the fears of Cuban and Soviet designs among the nations in the Caribbean and Central American area. Efforts to capitalize on this through United States embassies in the area bore little fruit. Nations listened politely, agreed privately, but provided no visible show of concern. There were no known protests, either over the presence of the brigade or over the fact that, at the same time, Nicaragua sent its first arms purchasing mission to the Soviet Union.

The incident did serious damage to the image of the Carter administration at home. Tom Wicker, columnist for the *New York Times*, wrote on September 18:

> Jimmy Carter's Cuban fiasco, meanwhile, ranks right up there with the Dewey campaign of 1948 for snatching defeat from the jaws of victory. Anything short of Soviet capitulation not only will make Mr. Carter appear to have accepted a Soviet bridgehead in the Western Hemisphere; worse, a likely ratification of SALT II has been converted into possible defeat.[81]

Don Oberdorfer, writing retrospectively in the *Washington Post* on October 16, said:

> Whatever the view of the importance or unimportance of the Soviet "brigade," whether insiders or outsiders to the Carter administration, whether Carter friend or Carter foe, nearly all those familiar with the details of this latest Cuban crisis agree that it was badly mishandled.[82]

Could the results have been different? If there are answers, they lie in five aspects: the use of intelligence, the role of the Senate, the problems of executive pronouncements, suspicion of the Soviets, and the divergent voices of an administration.

The widespread knowledge of the capacity of American intelligence has had at least two results. It has created, particularly among members of Congress, an assumption of a far greater U.S. capacity to follow events around the world than is realistic. Additionally, regardless of whether the belief is correct, it provides a political issue for those who wish to seize upon it when it appears that there has been a "failure of intelligence."

In the assessment of this capacity, attention is seldom paid to the need for budgetary and staffing priorities, even in intelligence. After 1962, with the proliferation of other problems around the world, resources were taken from the observation of Cuba. Decisions were made that the priority in Cuba remained the monitoring of heavy weapons systems. Brigades were not on that list.

In this assessment, there is also little room for a fine appreciation of the capacities of different intelligence tools. Carter was criticized for suspending the SR-71 flights over Cuba; the failure to detect the brigade was attributed to this. The fact is that the monitoring of the type of information that led to "discovering" the brigade is not a function of the SR-71, but of other types of aircraft which do not need to overfly to achieve their mission.

The knowledge of intelligence capacity has also created a heavy demand for access to intelligence. With that goes the temptation to use sensitive information. The number of classified publications disseminating intelligence has increased substantially in twenty years.

Oberdorfer, in his October 16 roundup of the affair, reports that when Senator Stone was advised by an aide of the reports of a Soviet troop buildup, he asked whether the information was classified. The aide, reportedly, said it was not. Whatever the basis for that response, the information on which Stone acted was indeed highly classified; the temptation to use it was too great for Stone to be deterred by that fact.

The urge to use intelligence means that it is often used before it has been fully checked or evaluated. The intelligence on the unit in Cuba was gathered under the pressure of Stone's earlier inquiry and the known order from the White House to increase the information on Cuba. The instant that some new information was developed, the news spread through both official and congressional networks. There was little opportunity to check the antecedents of the brigade before it had become a public issue. Once that had happened, the possibility of diminishing the impact by revealing that such a unit had been there for seventeen years was substantially reduced. Early and partial disclosures may also dry up sources essential for the full story.

The role of two senators was obviously crucial in this episode. Each had a rationale for his actions. Senator Stone could claim a serious concern over national security in an area close to his constituency. Senator Church justified his action on the basis that an announcement of the existence of the brigade from some official source was preferable to a leak. While this was a debatable premise, it was a premise.

Questions have been raised about the timing and necessity of Under Secretary Newsom's call to Senator Church. No one knew or had a realistic possibility of finding out, at the time, if or when the story would leak. Senator Church would have been equally if not more disturbed to have read the item in the newspaper. His anger would have been compounded had he discovered that the administration already knew of the brigade and that another member of the Foreign Relations Committee had already been informed.

Might Church have been dissuaded from taking the position he did, that the brigade should be withdrawn? Possibly. There is little doubt, however, that he felt doubly stung, having been the one who issued the release denying Senator Stone's contention—as Church had issued a denial for Kennedy seventeen years before.

The expansion of the senatorial role in foreign affairs means that not only the Senate but individual senators are deeply involved. To some, like Senator Church, a liberal in a conservative state, that involvement is a political problem. Whatever the rationale given, the politics of senatorial survival—in Stone's case as well as that of Church—was a factor that the administration did not believe it could control, and did not attempt to control.

Senator Church and others asked why the administration did not announce the presence of the brigade, once its presence was established.

The question of what and when to announce has implications beyond the item being announced. Will an official announcement give the matter greater significance than it deserves? Since one is never certain how credible or effective a leak will be, is it asking for trouble to anticipate a leak? The general impression within the Department of State is that it is better to respond to questions on information such as this than to give such information the buildup and significance of an official announcement. Given the history of the brigade issue and the known senatorial interest, this judgment may have been wrong. But it was a close call.

Until the matter ballooned into a major issue, there was also the question of the basis for an official U.S. complaint to the Soviets. There were numerous conjectures regarding the purpose of the brigade: "to protect sensitive Soviet installations; tropical training; as a core group for force projections into the Latin region; as a defensive unit in case of a U.S. threat to Cuba; to protect Soviet nuclear weapons in case these should be introduced into Cuba."[83]

Had the administration had the luxury of time to seek further information, the handling of the results could have been different. Clearly an offensive role directed in any way against the United States would have been grounds for a strong protest. If, however, the unit had proven to be in Cuba for training purposes, the United States would have been hesitant to protest on any basis that would question the appropriateness of military training missions in other countries. As the Soviets pointed out, the United States has such training centers, too.

Even without the *Aviation Week* probe, the appropriateness of a volunteered announcement of the brigade by the executive would have been debated.

The brigade issue involved both the Soviet Union and Cuba, two countries toward which massive suspicion exists within the American public, Congress, and the executive. Under such circumstances, the administration was not in a position to accept, at face value, the Soviet response that this unit was part of a "training center." The political audience the administration faced assumed automatically that skulduggery was at work. Those who talked with the Soviets were required, if faithful to their instructions, to convey this view and to question the truth of the Soviet response. Questions were undoubtedly put that the Soviets believed to be inappropriate prying into their affairs and those of Cuba. That does not make for effective diplomacy, particularly where the Soviet answer may be the correct one.

The problem was compounded by different views within the administration. The view of Secretary Vance was that it was desirable to reach with the Soviets the most acceptable outcome possible in order to permit the resumption of the SALT ratification process. In the White House, some of the president's closest associates saw the brigade issue as a basis for strengthening the president's image as a tough leader and reminding the region of the perfidy of the Soviets. To some, SALT was a less desirable objective. Others argued that tough action on the president's part would permit a politically strengthened Carter to tell the Senate that the Russian brigade had been neutralized and to ask for the approval of SALT.[84]

Another school of thought rejected the acceptance of the unit as a training unit on the grounds that to permit the Soviets to train Cubans for external adventures was an even greater threat to U.S. interests than if the unit were there purely as a Soviet brigade.

The Soviets were most certainly aware of the different points of view. Georgi Arbatov, head of Moscow's Institute on the USA and Canada, was quoted as saying:

> The issue raises many doubts about the goals of American policy, what the Americans are up to, what they do want, how you understand this vacillation in their policy and whether they really are partners with whom you can do this tremendously important job of lessening world tensions.[85]

Perhaps the brigade affair was mismanaged. A valid case can be made that the administration misjudged the full potential impact of the issue when it first emerged in July. Despite public disclosure, there was little public or congressional attention. A more precise recollection of Senator Church's experience during the Kennedy administration might have made the secretary and the under secretary more cautious about approaching him in the middle of a political campaign in Idaho. Secretary Vance gambled, in his use of the words "status quo," that the Soviets were still sufficiently interested in preserving the SALT treaty that they would, once more, help an American administration out of a domestic dilemma. He lost the gamble. It is difficult, however, to see what realistic alternatives he might have had. Perhaps the problem is much deeper; it is certainly not confined to a single administration.

The proliferation of access to sophisticated and often partial intelligence means that sensitive information can be released without satisfactory evaluation or the opportunity to judge its total impact on the nation's foreign policy. Had it been possible to ask the Soviets about the brigade, as Marshall Shulman did of Bessmertnykh, and to receive and study the reply away from the glare of public pressure, many of the serious effects of this episode might have been avoided.

The two senators who played the key roles in this affair were both members of the president's party. Fundamental to the politics of the United States, however, is the fact that the constituency of members of Congress prevails over party responsibility. Senator Church could argue that he consulted Secretary Vance before making the announcement and that he tried to reach President Carter. Both are true. Neither, however, removes the fact that Senator Church, in the last analysis, had to consider his political position in Idaho and the effect of the brigade issue on his bid for reelection. It is conceivable that that concern took precedence over his concern about U.S.–U.S.S.R. relations.

Once the matter became an issue, unrealistic burdens were placed on diplomacy. Secretary Vance was required to assume, from the outset, that the Soviet response was incorrect. He was required to seek changes, not to lessen a threat but to meet the needs of American politics. His mission was not to resolve a problem through seeking an explanation; it was to resolve, through diplomacy with the Soviets, an American domestic issue. Few countries, and least of all the Soviets, willingly help other nations out of political dilemmas if it involves what they consider retreats or sacrifices.

While it is possible to argue that the escalating involvement of President Carter in this issue and the general consistency of his approach were appropriate, his public image was one of uncertainty and lack of clear purpose. For this, any president must to some extent bear the responsibility. President Carter was not alone among presidents who were reluctant to rein in the expressions of separate views and separate nuances by close members of their circles.

The affair of the Soviet brigade deserves study, not as a strange aberration in American foreign policy but as an example of the serious dangers to a democracy of the casual use of intelligence, the independent objectives of key lawmakers, the unrealistic expectations of diplomacy, and the excessive presidential tolerance of diverse public expressions.

In the end, everyone lost. The possibility of a strategic arms limitation treaty was lost to both the Soviets and the United States. The United States appeared inept, not only to the rest of the world, but to its closest allies. The Carter administration lost the election. And the two senators, who acted as they did in part because they were facing elections, were defeated.

APPENDIX A

Department of State
Daily Press Briefing
Friday, 31 August 1979
Subject—Cuba: Soviet Troops, Non-Aligned Summit

On August 31, Hodding Carter, Assistant Secretary of State for Public Affairs, read the prepared statement on the Soviet brigade in Cuba at the daily noon press briefing in the Department of State. He was questioned at length by the press on various aspects of the affair. Excerpts follow:

The Mission

Q Hodding, why are you concerned?

A Our concern is centered on the fact that these are, in fact, combat troops, and that it is difficult to understand the rationale for their presence.

Q Well, do you think they are there as a staging area for something else?

A I have no way to determine at this point the brigade's mission, this unit's mission. This is among the things we are seeking to determine.

Q When you called in the Soviet Charge two days ago, what did he say about it? What do you think is the rationale behind doing that at this time?

A I can't go into our diplomatic exchanges. Let me just go on to reiterate that we will continue our discussions on this. I expect more. I would not look to a great deal from that first discussion. But we are continuing them.

Q Hodding, in that discussion with the Soviet Charge, can you tell us, did we go beyond asking for an explanation, (a) did we receive one, and (b) beyond that, did we ask for the removal of any or part of this combat unit?

A I am really not going to be able to go any further into the subject of the conversation or the response except to say that we intend to continue pursuing the matter.

.   .   .   .

Soviet Bases

Now, the President has stated, as he reiterated as recently as a letter within the month, that it is the policy of the United States to oppose any efforts, direct or indirect, by the Soviet Union to establish military bases in the Western Hemisphere. That remains the policy.

What is not at this point clear is a way to characterize the presence of this combat unit.

Q Hodding, can I please follow that?

I am trying to figure out what you are saying.

Are you saying that if, in fact, this unit does not constitute a base or is not directed towards the establishment of a base, then we have no right or jurisdiction to ask them to remove these forces?

A I am really not going to try to speculate on it. I am telling you what is the context of our agreement with them, insofar as the 1960 and 1970 affirmations go. However, that aside, we are naturally concerned about the presence of Soviet combat troops in Cuba.

Q But you cannot say here that we have asked them either to reduce the number or to take those troops home?

I mean, I find that incredible.

A Well, that is what you are going to have to find it, in that I am not going to say here what it is that we have done, except to raise this subject with them, and the fact that we are actively pursuing it.

.   .   .   .

Soviet Troop Strength

Q My understanding was that up until very recently—within the last week or two—when asked about this by Senator Stone and others, the Department of Defense and the State Department were saying that there appeared to be 2,000 Cuban troops or Soviet troops who were acting in an advisory capacity, plus a command structure.

Now you say there are about maybe as many as 5,000 Soviet military personnel and that there is a combat brigade.

Were these people moved in in the last two weeks? Or is this something that comes about as a result of a reevaluation of intelligence?

A Let me repeat that we have had indications of some elements of what now has taken shape from our analysis since 1976. During that time we have been developing information about it. We have recently come to the unambiguous conclusion that such a unit was on the ground.

Q How can there have been an increase of 3,000 in your estimate of the number of Soviet troops?

A Well, to begin with, it is not even by your figures 3,000.

Q Well, 2,000 then.

A Second, it is, as we all know, a function of intelligence—as you discovered in other areas over the last some months—not to be able to say with precision in this kind of unit the number of folk that are there. It requires repeated analysis and information.

I am not really going to go any further into the intelligence methods, however.

.   .   .   .

Q And also a month ago, in a letter to Stone, the Secretary said that over the past several years there is no evidence of any substantial increase of Soviet military presence in Cuba over the last several years or of the presence of a Soviet military base; there is no significant Soviet forces in Cuba.

Was that statement correct at the time he made it?

A It certainly was. It was based on the best evidence that was available to this nation at that time that that letter was written.

Q It is a big build-up.

A No.

Q Either that or we didn't know what was going on. Isn't that the conclusion, Hodding?

A I think that, again, as with all of this, except in Superman fantasies, the way this thing is put together requires continual analysis and re-analysis of information available from a number of sources. You begin to build a picture, and that picture changes over time.

.   .   .   .

MIG-23s

Q One more thing: What happened to those MIG-23s? Can you just refresh our memory on the MIG-23s earlier in the year where we had a lot of controversy?

A The last thing that I can tell you on that was the Q and A we developed with you on January 17, 1979. I have a copy of it here. I think the operative sentence here was, ''Our current assessment based on our ongoing examination is that the MIG-23 aircraft now in Cuba do not constitute an offensive threat to the United States.'' It went on to say that, ''We do not think at this time it constitutes a violation of a 1962 agreement''—I said 1960 earlier—''nor is there any indication that they [are] configured to carry nuclear weapons or that there are any nuclear weapons on Cuba.''

We went on to say, ''The transfer of those aircraft was a matter of importance to us,'' that we had raised it directly with the Soviets, and so forth; it also said that we would continue to keep the situation under review.

Q I would assume that that is still valid?

A Yes.

Q — that assessment?

A Yes, it is.

Q — that there are no nuclear weapons in Cuba now?

A Yes.

Q Those are 20 planes? How many planes?

A Bernie, I don't know that I have that in this clip. . . . There had been MIG-23s there before. I do not have the number of that in front of me.

.   .   .   .

U.S. Reaction

Q Can you confirm today that it is a goal of U.S. foreign policy to seek the removal of these Soviet troops? And if not, will we be satisfied to have 5,000 Soviet troops in Panama, Nicaragua, and so on?

A Let me simply say that we are raising this because the presence of combat troops is a matter of concern. It will continue to be. I'm not going to talk with you as to, you know, what is acceptable, under what form, and how. We are going to pursue this matter, and we are actively pursuing it. What happens next, we will see.

Q Let me ask a follow-up on that, then. In connection with diplomatic measures to pursue whatever our policy is, with respect to whatever removal efforts we aim at, you, as I interpret your remark, [distance] SALT from involvement. Would we consider other matters such as JFK considered and execute a blockade? Or more generally, in the Carter Administration are all aspects of the Monroe Doctrine dead? If they aren't, which aspects are still alive?

A If you are asking specifically what contingencies we have in mind if a speculative situation arose, I would have to say we would have to deal with that situation when it arose, and I wouldn't talk about contingencies.

Q But this isn't speculative. They are there.

A Wait a minute. If you're asking me to repeat myself about the concern we feel about what is a serious situation, then I will repeat that concern and tell you that we are raising it because we view it as a serious matter; but I'm not really going to speculate with you as to what we might do.

I was rereading the transcript on the Kennedy thing, as a matter of fact, and one of the interesting aspects of it that I would remind all of you is that for eleven days you were shut out entirely and there was a great deal of complaint about the operation of both Mr. Sylvester and Mr. Manning, who had my job then, in making sure you weren't informed as this thing progressed.

The reason the President gave in his press conference for not doing it was precisely not to deal with questions such as you're asking me right now while he was in the middle of a diplomatic negotiation. We are in the middle of a diplomatic negotiation. A lot of this, we are just simply not going to be able to deal with.

. . . . .

Unit Designation

Q Hodding, has your intelligence identified this Russian brigade? In other words, does it have a name, a number? And, secondly, what is the State Department's thinking as to what might motivate the Soviet's not bringing in three more brigades, for instance, in view of the fact that we have expressed our concern about Cuban troops all over the world for about two years, and not a thing has happened except they keep going around the world?

A Let me say on the latter, that is what we are pursuing now. I can't really answer the question because I don't know.

On the former, let me just say ON BACKGROUND, a brigade is just simply not a standard Soviet organization. It is something that is put together very rarely, very rarely. It is not a normal military configuration.

Q It has no identity. In other words, it's just a whole bunch of troops thrown in; right?

A It is an organizational principle very rarely used, so rarely that it hardly ever shows up at all.

Q You're calling it a brigade.

A Well, I'm trying not to. It is a loose term.

Q In the American concept a brigade is made up of two or [more] regiments.

A Forget the American concept. It is simply a term—I'm staying ON BACKGROUND here—which is very rarely used, just sometimes [for] organizational reasons that frankly are confusing to us.

.   .   .   .

OAS/Non-Aligned Conference

Q On the OAS and the Non-Aligned Conference, are any of the Hemispheric neighbors—have any of them expressed enough concern or has the United States in its contact with them discovered enough concern that this might be raised by any of the OAS members who are members of the Non-Aligned Conference at that meeting?

A Look, let me just say this: This is information that we have recently—a conclusion to which we have recently come. It has been obviously closely held, given the nature of the information; and I seriously doubt that we have raised it just up until now with anybody else other than those who have the forces there.

Q On that same point, do any of the assessments to which you are privy connect the presence or the stationing of these troops there at this time with the Non-Aligned Conference?

A I really wouldn't have any speculation to offer you on why, where, timing, any of that.

Q Did you say that at this time it doesn't have anything to do, as far as timing—this statement—with non-aligned countries?

A Oh, absolutely.

Q However, you say that it has become necessary for you to make the statement. Can you elaborate on that?

A Yes. Information was coming out in bits and pieces, and it seemed necessary to try to put out as fully as we could what it is we believed and what it was we were trying to do about it. It's an obligation in this case that we thought we owed to the people, to ourselves, and to the Congress.

.   .   .   .

Senator Stone

Q Hodding, what is the Secretary's reaction to Senator Stone? Is he grateful that the Senator expressed serious concern about this in contrast to what appears to be a signal failure of our intelligence services?

A No. You see—

Q Why not?

A I just would have to tell you that it is the usefulness of the intelligence services and their capacity to determine the truth. You don't really think there's some independent intelligence source of information that's been putting this stuff out.

Q There's a terrible lack of intelligence.

A Well then, all I can say is—

Q If a Senator from Florida expresses his deep concern so long ago and was sent one of those beautiful letters from the Secretary of State that all is well, and then we discover that all is not well and a combat unit is there, it would appear to me that Senator Stone is more intelligent than our intelligence. Am I wrong, Hodding?

A I would say there's a parallel between the two. In any case he's perfectly happy that the Senator pursued this matter fully.

. . . .

Q Can you tell us if this increasing trend of Soviet presence in Cuba has been an element in the decision of the Secretary to give more importance to Caribbean affairs? He announced that here recently.

A You mean the various stories stating his apparent feelings on the subject of Central America and what have you?

Let me say there are a number of factors that go into that. Obviously the economic difficulties of a number of the countries in the area; difficulties in terms of the political instability which face some of them. It is a complex of forces that raise a concern, and our desire to play a useful role there in meeting those concerns.

I would not try to single out any element alone and say that's the reason for it.

Q Hodding, two things: No. 1, you didn't say how the troops were quartered, but do you know geographically where they are in the country? Are they all around Havana, or are they spread out in the country?

A I don't have anything to offer you on that.

Q No. 2, in the Secretary's letter to Senator Stone on July 27 he said, "The President raised the question of the Soviet presence in Cuba with President Brezhnev in Vienna and made clear to him that a Soviet buildup would adversely affect our relationship." How will this Soviet buildup adversely affect the U.S. relationship with the Soviet Union?

A I think I'll let the President's statement there speak for itself, as to what affect we would see.

Q Will there be some change in the American relationship with the Soviet Union?

A I'm not going to be able to speculate on that.

Q Will you take the question as to what is a military base, since your whole discussion this morning appears to be revolving about the issue of—

A No. What I am saying is it doesn't revolve around that. The concern starts with the fact of combat troops, whether or not it constitutes a base or not.

The statement of American policy, which is of a kin to 1962 and 1970 statements, has to do with the military base in the Hemisphere.

Q But they are in violation then, if I understood your comments correctly. If they have established a base, they are in violation of earlier agreements.

A We will deal with all that when we get to it. But I am saying, in any case, we start with a concern about the combat troops.

Q Hence you come back to the question, how can we talk on equal terms if we don't understand what you mean by "base?"

A I think that is determined by what we are going to continue to explore with other parties on this matter.

Q So, you decline to explain.

A To go any further, sure.

APPENDIX B

Press Conference
Secretary of State Cyrus R. Vance
5 September 1979

SECRETARY VANCE: Good morning.

Before taking your questions I have a brief opening statement.

Let me begin with a few comments on the presence of a Soviet combat brigade in Cuba. We regard this as a very serious matter affecting our relations with the Soviet Union. The presence of this unit runs counter to long-held American policies.

The identification of this unit as a combat force has recently been confirmed by our intelligence community. They have now concluded that this force has been in Cuba since at least the mid-1970's. Re-analysis of the older, fragmentary data in the light of more recently acquired information suggests that elements of a Soviet brigade may have been there since the early 1970's, and possibly before that. The process of re-analyzing our earlier information continues.

The unit appears to consist of 2,000 to 3,000 personnel. It includes motorized rifle battalions, tank and artillery battalions, and combat and service support units. These figures are separate from the Soviet military advisory and technical military personnel in Cuba, which we now estimate to be between 1,500 and 2,000.

The specific mission of the combat unit is unclear. There is no air or sealift capability associated with the brigade which would give it an assault capability, nor is the presence of this unit covered by our bilateral understandings with the Soviets in 1962 or 1970.

Nonetheless, the presence of a Soviet combat unit in Cuba is a matter of serious concern.

I will be pursuing this matter with the Soviets in the coming days.

I will be discussing this issue with the Senate Foreign Relations Committee this afternoon and setting forth the approach which we plan to take with the Soviets. We will keep the press and the public informed to the fullest extent that we can as we proceed. I know you will understand that the interests of our country would not be served by my now going into the specific nature of our approach.

QUESTION: Two questions: First, have you or will you ask the Soviets to remove those troops? And how do you think this all will affect the national debate on SALT?

SECRETARY VANCE: On the first question, the discussions with the Soviets will affect the action which we will take.

Let me say very simply that I will not be satisfied with maintenance of the status quo.

And your second question?

QUESTION: How will this affect the national debate on SALT and other aspects of U.S.-Soviet relations?

SECRETARY VANCE: As I have indicated, this is a serious matter and will be treated as such. At the same time, SALT is a matter of fundamental importance.

I believe that the hearings on SALT ratification should proceed. However, we will be keeping in close touch with the Senate Committee and the members of the Senate as we proceed in our discussions with the Soviets.

QUESTION: Mr. Vance, how could the Soviets have stationed a brigade of this size and this caliber in Cuba for several years without U.S. intelligence finding out about it? And how does that reflect upon the ability of the intelligence community to monitor Soviet activities relating to SALT over a much broader land area in the Soviet Union?

SECRETARY VANCE: First, the information which has been assembled over a period of years has been fragmentary and it is very difficult to piece together.

As you know, in evaluating intelligence information, it is like putting a jigsaw puzzle together and one has to continue to examine the various fragments. And sometimes the fragments all fall together and then you can arrive at a conclusion. This is what happened in this case.

As to your second question, would you repeat it?

QUESTION: How does the inability of the intelligence community to detect this Soviet brigade for several years reflect upon its ability to detect small differences in Soviet rocket configurations and other SALT related intelligence problems on a much broader land area in the Soviet Union?

SECRETARY VANCE: There is a clear difference between determining whether a particular unit or element of a unit is, when covered by photographic intelligence from a satellite, a unit which belongs to a particular country, such as the Soviet Union, as opposed to the Cubans. This is much more difficult to monitor than monitoring such things as the establishment of new missile sites, [or] receiving an analysis of telemetry and the kinds of things which are important for SALT monitoring.

QUESTION: Mr. Secretary, if I may follow up on your response that you will not be satisfied with the status quo?

Is it the combat characteristics of this unit that are so disturbing to us or is it the presence of the forces?

In other words, are you or will we call for the removal of the forces themselves?

SECRETARY VANCE: It is the combat nature of the units which is a matter of very serious concern to us. We have realized, as you all know, that there were training units and signal units stationed there over a considerable period of time.

QUESTION: Mr. Secretary, something you said earlier implied to me at least that you may with time reconsider the question of linkage between SALT and whatever action you may request from the Soviets regarding the removal or reduction or whatever of these Soviet troops.

Am I hearing you wrong?

SECRETARY VANCE: What is said, Mr. Trewitt, is that I think that the hearings on ratification should go forward because of their fundamental importance. I have also said, however, because this is a matter of a serious nature, that we must keep in close contact and in discussion with members of the Senate as we go forward in our discussions with the Soviets.

QUESTION: Mr. Secretary, Senator Stone recently said that everything is not yet out; there is more to come.

Some of us have been told that the Soviets have constructed a military airfield and have been working on a missile boat base and that there might be even another base with combat troops.

Can you address that?

And, secondly, on the matter of the intelligence just becoming known, some of us were told last month, before you wrote your letter saying to the Senator there was no significant Soviet military force other than the advisers, we were told that there was intelligence, at least in July, to suggest very strongly that they had combat infantry artillery battalions there.

SECRETARY VANCE: Let me say at the time that I wrote my letter to Senator Stone, I reviewed this within the government with full interagency coordination among all of the intelligence elements of the government. At that time they concluded that there was not sufficient evidence to conclude that there was a combat presence in there.

I told Senator Stone after I wrote him the letter that we were going to intensify our investigation and collection activities and our analysis of the information as it came in, and that as soon as we felt that we had additional information which might bear on the subject and give us a clearer reading of what the situation was, I would immediately make this information available to him, to members of the relevant Senate Committees and others. And that is just what we have done.

QUESTION: Has the public been told the full story of Soviet military activity in Cuba?

SECRETARY VANCE: I think we have told the public everything at this point that is of significance. We are continuing to investigate other matters as well. And if we get information that is of importance, we will, of course, make it available.

QUESTION: Mr. Secretary, to move the matter to a slightly different area, as we all know, action has been taken against the CIA acting through journalists abroad. But there is another matter of interest, which is foreign intelligence services using the media in this country. And specifically I would like to ask if anything can or will be done about the case of the Mossad working through certain newspapers, including the *New York Times*, through certain agents, including Roy Cohn—and this has all been publicly documented—and through the old Permindex assassination network at this point to set up an assassination of Presidential candidate Lyndon LaRouche and possibly others as well? And isn't it time that we started cleaning up these kinds of rather filthy foreign operations?

SECRETARY VANCE: Well, I think you are leaping to conclusions on some of the matters that you have referred to. I do not want to endorse or give any credence to the allegations which you have made.

We will continue to pursue our activity in following the activities of any foreign intelligence agencies in the United States. But there is nothing more that I can add at this point to your statement.

QUESTION: Mr. Secretary, (1) do you consider what the Soviets have in Cuba as a base? And, (2) I am not quite sure how to ask this, but if they had been there for several years, have had a combat capability or a combat unit there for several years, why is it a serious matter?

SECRETARY VANCE: Let me answer the second half of your question first. The presence of combat troops in Cuba, Soviet combat troops, at any time, is a serious matter. And if we had known about that fact and could have demonstrated that fact in the mid-1970's or in the early 1970's, that would have been a serious factor then and would have been raised at that time as a serious matter to be dealt with.

Now, with respect to the question of whether or not the presence of these forces constitutes a base, the answer I must give you on that one is a very simple and straightforward one: We do not know at this time whether it constitutes a base. Our conversations and discussions with the Soviet Union will shed light on this, and we will have to arrive at our conclusion as we proceed with those discussions.

QUESTION: Mr. Secretary, early on in this Administration the United States, as a gesture of good will to the Cubans, cut off surveillance flights, specifically U-2 flights.

I am just wondering if you can tell us whether these were reinstated and, secondly, whether the lack of those surveillance flights may have contributed to the lack of information that you have had over the past couple of years.

SECRETARY VANCE: No. I don't think so. I think that the flights which were conducted have been sufficient—as one goes back and goes over the take that has come from those flights—to, in hindsight, as the final pieces fell into place which made it possible to come to this conclusion, on re-analysis, to take a look at the past information and conclude that that information—now that we have the final piece or two which puts the jigsaw together—to give you the conclusion that we have now arrived at.

QUESTION: Could I just follow up?

SECRETARY VANCE: Go ahead.

QUESTION: I am wondering on what basis you can now be so certain that those troops were introduced in the mid- or possibly even in the early '70's when for so many years you apparently did not have sufficient information to even respond.

SECRETARY VANCE: Because we have corroborating evidence of different kinds now that we did not have before.

QUESTION: What I am asking, sir, is in response to some of the questions that were raised in July, both your office and that of the Secretary of Defense were not even allowing the possibility of the presence of Soviet troops. It was being flatly denied at that time.

SECRETARY VANCE: That was the conclusion, at that point, of the intelligence community. Since then, as I said, additional evidence has become available, evidence which was redundant but backed up and corroborated other types of evidence. And once that pattern was put together, then the intelligence community was able to come to a firm conclusion.

QUESTION: Mr. Secretary, on that same question, do I understand you correctly to be saying that the 2,000 to 3,000-man brigade essentially was in place in Cuba before even this Administration took office?

SECRETARY VANCE: A force of approximately that size was, yes. That is the conclusion that has now been arrived at.

QUESTION: So all that has happened in the last few weeks is that the intelligence community has now reached that conclusion. The Soviets haven't done anything special in the last year or two?

SECRETARY VANCE: That is correct.

QUESTION: Mr. Secretary, is there any reason now why the 1962 agreement with the Russians at the time of the Cuban missile crisis could not be made public so that people would have a way of knowing whether the Russians are keeping that agreement or not?

SECRETARY VANCE: Well, the essence of the 1962 agreement is generally known to the public, and let me give you as much as I can about it. The 1962 agreement is not just a simple piece of paper. It consists of an exchange of letters between President Kennedy and Chairman Khrushchev; it consists of discussions between Russian officials, including Minister Kuznetsov, Minister Mikoyan, and individuals in the United States and representatives of the United States Government. It includes discussions between officials of the United States and Ambassador Dobrynin. So that it is a series of both exchanges of letters and discussions that make up the total agreement.

QUESTION: Why couldn't that whole package be made public now? What is the reason that it can't be made public? Seventeen years have passed.

SECRETARY VANCE: This is a matter which I think is a fair question to ask. We are reviewing the situation to determine whether or not we can at least put out a full summary of what the essense of that agreement and the agreement of 1970 is as well, and I hope that we may be able to do so.

QUESTION: Mr. Secretary, are there any plans by the U.S. Government to reinforce ground forces and Air Force units in Guantanamo at this time?

SECRETARY VANCE: I don't want to go into any actions which we might take in the future. Let me say, however, that is not to be taken in any way as an indication that we are planning to do that.

QUESTION: Mr. Secretary, did the re-analysis of the Cuban data follow the Nicaraguan—I'm sorry, the insurrection in Nicaragua by the Cuban-backed—

SECRETARY VANCE: It was not—

QUESTION: No correlation?

SECRETARY VANCE: It was not sparked in any way by that. This analysis was going on as a result of the reevaluation that we had been involved in; and as soon as we got the necessary information to arrive at the conclusions, we immediately released the conclusions.

QUESTION: Do you have any comment on the thesis that this is essentially a hand-holding operation for the Cubans who have forces around the world?

SECRETARY VANCE: There are many different theories as to what the purpose of the maintenance of that battalion or brigade in Cuba is. At this point, we do not know which of these various hypotheses is correct. Obviously, one of the issues which we will be discussing with the Soviets is the statement by the Soviets with respect to the purpose and intentions which relate to the brigade.

QUESTION: In view of the fact that another U.S. Ambassador had met several times with PLO officials, why was Ambassador Young singled out for holding a session with that group's U.N. representative, particularly since Young's action could have been justified by the fact that he was then President of the Security Council?

SECRETARY VANCE: Insofar as the situation of Ambassador Young's resignation is concerned, let me say several things: First, the situation has been gone into at length. The situation has been reviewed time and again by the Spokesman for the Department, and I wish to make very clear that I stand behind the statements of the Spokesman with respect to this matter.

I want to also make very clear that I stand fully behind the statement which I issued at the time that Andy's resignation was offered and accepted—namely, that Andy has made great contributions to the United States and to its foreign policy.

I think that it would not do any good—it would be fruitless, and indeed an unwise step—to rehash all of this ground again.

QUESTION: Mr. Secretary, it has now been a full week since the Soviet Charge d'Affaires was called in to the State Department and informed of American concern over the Soviet troops in Cuba. During that time, the only public response from the Soviets has been a rather scoffing one in the press. I understand further that the Soviet Charge's response was similar. Do you consider at this time that the Soviet response has been timely and serious?

SECRETARY VANCE: I have asked Ambassador Dobrynin to return at the earliest possible moment, and I will then be meeting with him. I do not feel, until I have had a chance to meet with him, that we will have had a serious chance to discuss this issue.

QUESTION: When do you expect that, sir?

SECRETARY VANCE: I don't know exactly. I will get a response, I hope, today to the message which I sent to him in regard to his return.

QUESTION: You seemed to imply earlier, in response to Mr. Wallach, that it is the combat nature of the Soviet force that bothers us, and to me, at any rate, implied that the men can stay if the combat nature of the force is removed. Is that what you meant to imply?

SECRETARY VANCE: What I meant to say is that the combat nature is of great importance. It is of serious concern to us. I want to have further discussions about this whole matter, including the purpose and intention of the presence of the brigade. I don't want to, at this point, comment any further than I have already about the matter of what we will do.

QUESTION: Can I follow that? What impact do you think they have, whatever their purpose is down there? What impact does their presence have on problems that are already under way in the region?

SECRETARY VANCE: On the—

QUESTION: What impact does the presence of Soviet troops in Cuba have on problems in the Caribbean and in Central America?

SECRETARY VANCE: I don't think we have any evidence at this point as to what the impact may or may not be. One can speculate on what the impact might be, depending upon the situation, the facts, and what their purpose is. But it would be, I think, fruitless for me to speculate.

QUESTION: Mr. Secretary, North Korea has rejected the joint United States and South Korean proposal for three-way talks. What is the next United States step toward North Korea?

SECRETARY VANCE: Our position is that we shall watch and wait and see what happens. I do not necessarily consider the response which has been given by the North Koreans as the final response, and therefore we will wait and watch and see what happens.

QUESTION: Mr. Secretary, will the United States reconsider its contacts with the PLO in light of Foreign Minister Dayan's contacts? Is the United States seeking a release from its commitments? And, thirdly, is a summit on the Middle East planned here in the autumn, and if so, why?

SECRETARY VANCE: There are no plans at this point to have a summit here in the autumn. I think, as you know, Minister Dayan and I believe Minister Ali will be coming here later this month to discuss with us the situation relating to the monitoring force for the withdrawal from the Sinai. That is the only meeting that is planned at this time.

Turning to Minister Dayan's meetings, those meetings were with individuals located in the West Bank and Gaza. It has always been clear from the outset that insofar as discussions with Palestinians living on the West Bank and Gaza were concerned, both the Israelis and the U.S. could have discussions with them because this would be both helpful and useful in connection with the negotiations which are going forward with respect to the autonomy negotiations or the so-called West Bank/Gaza negotiations.

QUESTION: Mr. Secretary, a series of situations and reports, since we last met in this room several months ago, have raised a question about your willingness to continue in this job; and some of them in recent days have even raised questions about your authority to continue as the man in charge of United States foreign policy. I would like to ask you, have you considered resigning, other than this mass resignation which took place some time ago? And is there any doubt in your mind, or have you taken up the matter, about your authority over United States foreign policy?

SECRETARY VANCE: I had an idea somebody might raise a question like this.

First, insofar as what I have done, let me say very clearly that these kinds of stories arise time and time again with anybody in this job. These kinds of stories go with the job. I am not losing any sleep about this, and I would advise you not to lose any sleep about it.

On the other question, with respect to authority, I have the responsibility under the President for the development and implementation of the foreign policy of the United States, and that includes all aspects of that policy. I will do just that, and I will continue to do so.

QUESTION: Mr. Secretary, back to the Cuban thing. What particularly prompted this re-analysis? I'm not certain whether Senator Stone's charges or what particularly came to your attention, and when, actually, did this re-analysis take place?

SECRETARY VANCE: The re-analysis was done in the early part of July, as I recall it—maybe even late June. There was some additional information which was again fragmentary, and on the basis of that, as I recall it, it was determined that we should do a re-analysis. We, subsequently, as I recall it, had conversations with Senator Stone and with others, and we indicated to them that we planned to not only do our re-analysis but to intensify our efforts just to make sure that there wasn't something that we were missing. That's how the process got started and continued.

QUESTION: Sir, what is the matter with the United States and Mexico? Why can't we get along? We seem to have broken down on negotiations on gas and illegal aliens and the oil spill. What's the matter?

SECRETARY VANCE: Well, we really haven't broken down on negotiations with respect to gas. Let me start with that. Mr. Christopher went down to Mexico recently to continue the negotiations—they are very difficult negotiations—and in the process of two days of talks, they were able to make further progress. However, important differences remained. It's a tough negotiation; there isn't any doubt about it. And just because you can't reach agreement in several sessions doesn't mean you give up. They are not broken off. They are going to continue, and they will continue.

Insofar as the question of undocumented workers is concerned, those discussions are proceeding at a pace and in a fashion which is satisfactory to both of our countries, and we will be continuing to press forward with those.

Insofar as the oil spill is concerned, the problem of the oil spill is one of those events that happens in the relationships between two countries. We, quite properly, have raised this question with them. They are considering the matter. They have matters which they would like to raise of a similar nature, going back into the past, with respect to some problems that were raised from the rivers and waters that flowed from the United States into Mexico. These are the kind of problems that we as neighbors and allies and friends will be able to discuss and work out; and therefore, I really cannot accept your overly alarmist views of a breakdown of relations.

The President and President Lopez Portillo will be meeting around the 28th of September to go forward with the meeting which they had planned. This is part of a series of meetings. They have many things to discuss, and I look forward to, I believe, a good and constructive meeting. I know that's the way we view it, and I believe it's the way the Mexicans view it.

QUESTION: Mr. Secretary, on Friday Senator Stone said that the presence of the Russian troops in Cuba was of the same gravity as the 1962 Cuban missile crisis confrontation. Number one, do you believe that that is a correct assessment? And number two, if it is, is the United States making any contingency plans for reactions that would be of the same gravity as we took in 1962?

SECRETARY VANCE: Let me say I wish to repeat that I believe this to be a serious matter. However, it does not involve, as did the 1962 missile crisis, the question of offensive nuclear weapons. So there is a vast difference between the two. However, that does not mean that it is not a serious matter.

QUESTION: Mr. Secretary, in the wake of Ambassador Young's resignation, there was a sudden rise in tensions between the black and Jewish community in the United States, and some black leaders talked about the fact of there being a perception in the street that either the American Jewish community or Israel was behind the Young resignation. I would like to ask you, sir, what is the Administration view? Was the Young resignation brought about in fact by the American Jewish community or Israel, or was it brought about as a result of his own actions, or whatever, sir?

SECRETARY VANCE: Let me say that in my judgment it was not the result of actions by the Jewish community. I want to make that very clear, and I think that I have spoken to the rest of the question.

QUESTION: On the matter of the role of intelligence in forging foreign and national security policy, I would like your observations. It seems to me sometimes we make the policy, and then go get the intelligence. I'm thinking of North Korea, when the army, after the President made his policy of withdrawing the troops, the army went back on a zero-based intelligence analysis, started from scratch and found out there were a hell of a lot more troops there than they had thought. We seem to be doing the same thing on Cuba. We lifted the U–2 or SR–71 aircraft flights as a gesture of good will, and then a year or so later we discover Soviet combat troops.

Do you have any observation on that?

SECRETARY VANCE: Yes. I think in the case of the Korean analysis which was done, the analysis was part of a continuing review process that goes on in the intelligence community with respect to the threat that is posed to our forces and the forces of our allies; and this was part of an ongoing process that had been going for a long period of time. And again in that case, as one went forward, bits of information as we proceeded over a period of years, starting back before this Administration, began to begin to build a pattern which was not at all clear when you first started picking up these bits and pieces of information. This is one of the problems particularly when you are dealing with ground units. It is a lot harder when you're dealing with ground units and that type of thing, than it is dealing with the kind of matters which are before you when you have to deal with the monitoring of a SALT agreement where you have large installations, large types of equipment like missiles. It is much easier to deal with a large missile than it is with a tank or even a number of tanks.

QUESTION: Mr. Secretary, as you know, Prime Ministers Lynch and Thatcher are meeting today. You or the Department recently suspended arms sales to the Royal Ulster Constabulary. In the meantime, people like Governor Carey have even stepped in to offer mediation. My question is, when will this study that you are doing now on this be completed, and are you contemplating suggesting to Mrs. Thatcher and the British Government a new political initiative to try and solve the problem?

SECRETARY VANCE: The answer is that we are not planning to suggest a new political initiative. Our position has been—and President Carter stated it very clearly in 1977—a position of impartiality. It is a position of condemning terrorism and violence, and it is a position which supports the bringing together of the various factions in an attempt to try and move toward a peaceful solution.

It's an immensely difficult problem, as all of us know—one of the most difficult of these types of problems that exist throughout the world.

The position which we have taken is supported by the British Government, by the Irish Government and by the political parties in both Ireland and Northern Ireland. For us to intrude ourselves at this point into the Irish situation, in my judgment, would not be wise. I think it would be resented by the parties concerned, and they are the ones that should deal with this issue.

QUESTION: Thank you, sir.

A P P E N D I X   C

Remarks by Zbigniew Brzezinski
National Security Adviser
September 7, 1979

*National Security Affairs Adviser Zbigniew Brzezinski made the following re-
marks at a meeting with out-of-town editors yesterday morning:*

Let me just make a few introductory remarks and then I am at your service to
answer any questions that you may wish to pose.

I think it is useful to note that the posturing of Cuba as a nonaligned country
is fundamentally ridiculous.

Castro is a puppet of the Soviet Union and we view him as such. Throughout
the world there isn't one instance in which Castro has deviated from official
Soviet policy in any respect whatsoever. Castro economically is totally dependent on subventions from the Soviet Union. The $3 billion annual Soviet eco-
nomic aid to Cuba represents one-quarter of Cuba's gross national product.

Soviet industrial projects in Cuba account for 30 percent of Cuba's electric
power output; 95 percent of Cuba's steel production; 100 percent of Cuba's
sheet metal output and the bulk of Cuba's sugar harvest mechanization; approximately three-fifths of Cuba's imports come from the Soviet Union; and so
does virtually all of Cuba's oil at a 40 percent discount from the average OPEC
prices.

The Soviet Union purchases 72 percent of all Cuban exports and arranges
for East European nations to buy Cuban sugar at prices well above world prices.
In fact, I wonder how the Jamaicans, for example, react to the fact that the
Cubans get five times over the world price for sugar.

Militarily, Cuba is entirely dependent on the Soviet Union. Soviet military
support for Cuba goes far beyond Cuba's defensive needs, as witnessed by the
fact that the large proportion of the military equipment supplied to Cuba is used
by Cubans in combat abroad and far from Cuba.

Source: *Washington Post*, Sept. 8, 1979, A8

The Soviet Union supplies to Cuba jet fighters, transports, submarines, missile patrol boats, attack helicopters and antisubmarine patrol boats.

Cuba provides the manpower and since 1975, it has been converting its armed forces from a primarily defensive role to one capable of offensive operations far from Cuban shores. In keeping with that, Cuba deploys forces—combat troops I mean—and advisers in Africa where it acts as a proxy for Soviet military intervention. It does so in the Horn of Africa, in the Yemen and elsewhere.

In effect, Cuba is an active surrogate for foreign policy which is not shaped by itself, and is paid for this by economic and military support on a scale that underlines Cuba's status as a dependent client of the Soviet Union.

A P P E N D I X   D

Text of Televised Remarks by President Carter
September 7, 1979

'We Are Confident Of Our Ability to Defend' the Nation

Here is the text of President Carter's speech yesterday on the presence of Soviet troops in Cuba:

I want to take a few minutes to speak to you about the presence of the Soviet combat brigade in Cuba.

The facts relating to this issue have been carefully laid out by Secretary [of State Cyrus] Vance, both in his public statement and in his testimony before the Congress.

The facts, in brief, are as follows:

We have concluded as the consequences of intensified intelligence efforts that a Soviet combat unit is currently stationed in Cuba. We have some evidence to indicate that such a unit has been in Cuba for some time, perhaps for quite a few years.

The brigade consists of 2,000 to 3,000 troops. It's equipped with conventional weapons such as about 40 tanks and some field artillery pieces and has conducted training as an organized unit. It is not an assault force. It does not have airlift or seagoing capabilities and does not have weapons capable of attacking the United States.

The purpose of this combat unit is not yet clear. However, the secretary of state spoke for me and for our nation on Wednesday when he said that we consider the presence of a Soviet combat brigade in Cuba to be a very serious matter and that this status quo is not acceptable.

We are confident about our ability to defend our country or any of our friends from external aggression. The issue posed is of a different nature. It involves the stationing of Soviet combat troops here in the Western Hemisphere, in a

Source: *Washington Post*, Sept. 8, 1979, A8

country which acts as a Soviet proxy in military adventures in other areas of the world like Africa.

We do have the right to insist that the Soviet Union respect our interests and our concerns if the Soviet Union expects us to respect their sensibilities and their concerns. Otherwise, relations between our two countries will inevitably be adversely affected.

We are seriously pursuing this issue with the Soviet Union and we are consulting closely with the Congress. Let me emphasize that this is a sensitive issue that faces our nation—all of us. And our nation as a whole must respond, not only with firmness and strength, but also with calm and a sense of proportion. This is a time for firm diplomacy, not panic and not exaggeration. As Secretary Vance discusses this issue with Soviet representatives in the coming days, the Congress and the American people can help to ensure a successful outcome of these discussions and negotiations by preserving an atmosphere in which our diplomacy can work.

I know I speak for the leadership in Congress with whom I have met this afternoon, as well as for my own administration, when I express my confidence that our nation can continue to show itself to be calm and steady as well as strong and firm.

Thank you very much.

APPENDIX E

Text of President Carter's Speech to the Nation October 1, 1979

For Immediate Release   October 1, 1979

Office of the White House Press Secretary

THE WHITE HOUSE

Remarks of the President
in an Address to the Nation

The Oval Office

9:00 P.M. EDT

Good evening.

I want to talk with you about a subject that is my highest concern, as it has been for every President. That subject is peace and the security of the United States.

We are at peace tonight, as we have been at peace throughout the time of my service in this office. The peace we enjoy is the peace of the strong. Our national defenses are unsurpassed in the world. Those defenses are stronger tonight than they were two years ago; and they will be stronger two years from now than they are tonight, because of carefully planned improvements that are going forward with your support and with the support of the Congress.

Our program for modernizing and strengthening the military forces of the NATO alliance is on track, with the full cooperation and participation of our European allies. Our strategic nuclear forces are powerful enough to destroy any potential adversary many times over, and the invulnerability of those forces will soon be further assured by a new system of powerful mobile missiles. These systems are designed for stability and defense.

Beyond these military defenses, we are on the threshold of a great advance in the control of nuclear weapons—the adoption of the second Strategic Arms Limitation Treaty, SALT II.

This evening, I also want to report to you about the highly publicized Soviet brigade in Cuba and about its bearing on the important relationship between our Nation and the Soviet Union.

This is not a simple or easy subject.

The United States and the Soviet Union are the two most powerful nations on earth, and the relationship between us is complex because it involves strong elements of both competition and cooperation.

Our fundamental philosophies conflict. Quite often, our national interests conflict as well. As two great nations, we do have common interests and we share an overwhelming mutual concern in preventing a nuclear war. We must recognize therefore that nuclear arms control agreements are vital to both our countries, and that we must also exercise self-restraint in our relations and be sensitive to each other's concerns.

Recently we obtained evidence that a Soviet combat brigade has been in Cuba for several years. The presence of Soviet combat troops in Cuba is of serious concern to us.

I want to reassure you at the outset that we do not face any immediate, concrete threat that could escalate into war or a major confrontation.

But we do face a challenge. It is a challenge to our wisdom—a challenge to our ability to act in a firm, decisive way without destroying the basis for cooperation that helps to maintain world peace and control nuclear weapons. It is a challenge to our determination to give a measured and effective response to Soviet competition and to Cuban military activities around the world.

Now let me explain the specific problem of the Soviet brigade and describe the more general problem of Soviet-Cuban military activism in the Third World.

Here is the background on Soviet forces in Cuba: As most of you know, 17 years ago in the era of the Cold War, the Soviet Union suddenly attempted to introduce offensive nuclear missiles and bombers into Cuba. This direct threat to the United States ended with the Soviet agreement to withdraw those nuclear weapons, and a commitment not to introduce offensive weapons into Cuba thereafter.

At the time of that 1962 missile crisis, there were more than 20,000 Soviet military personnel in Cuba. Most of them were withdrawn, and we monitored their departure. It was believed that those who stayed behind were not combat forces, but were there to advise and train Cubans and to perform intelligence functions.

Just recently American intelligence obtained persuasive evidence that some of these Soviet forces had been organized into a combat unit. When attention was then focused on a careful review of past intelligence data, it was possible for our experts to conclude that this unit had existed for several years, probably since the mid-1970s and possibly even longer.

This unit appears to be a brigade of two or three thousand men. It is armed with about 40 tanks and other modern military equipment. It has been organized as a combat unit. Its training exercises have been those of a combat unit.

This is not a large force, nor an assault force. It presents no direct threat to us. It has no airborne or seaborne capability. In contrast to the 1962 crisis, no nuclear threat to the United States is involved.

Nevertheless, this Soviet brigade in Cuba is a serious matter. It contributes to tension in the Caribbean and the Central American region. The delivery of modern arms to Cuba and the presence of Soviet naval forces in Cuban waters have strengthened the Soviet-Cuban military relationship. They had added to the fears of some countries that they may come under Soviet or Cuban pressure.

During the last few years, the Soviets have been increasing the delivery of military supplies to Cuba. The result is that Cuba now has one of the largest, best equipped armed forces in this region. These military forces are used to intrude into other countries in Africa and the Middle East.

There is a special relationship between Cuba and the Soviet Union. The Cubans get their weapons free. Other Soviet satellite countries have to pay for their military supplies.

The Communist regime in Cuba is an economic failure that cannot sustain itself. The Soviet Union must send to Cuba about $8 million in economic aid every day.

Fidel Castro does not pay money for Soviet arms; the Cuban people pay a much higher price. In every international dispute, on every international issue, the Cuban regime automatically follows the Soviet line.

The Soviet brigade is a manifestation of Moscow's dominance of Cuba. It raises the level of that dominance—and it raises the level of responsibility that the Soviet Union must take for escalating Cuban military actions abroad.

Now I want to report further on what we are doing to resolve these problems and to counter these activities.

Over the past three weeks, we have discussed this issue at great length with top Soviet officials.

We have made it clear that the presence of a Soviet combat unit in Cuba is a matter of serious concern to us. The Soviet Union does not admit that the unit in question is a combat unit. However, the Soviets have made certain statements to us with respect to our concern:

— That the unit in question is a training center, that it does nothing more than training, and can do nothing more;

— That they will not change its function or status as a training center. We understand this to mean that they do not intend to enlarge the unit or to give it additional capabilities;

— They have said that the Soviet personnel in Cuba are not and will not be a threat to the United States or to any other nation;

— That they reaffirm the 1962 understanding and the mutually agreed upon confirmation in 1970 and will abide by it in the future. We, for our part, reconfirm this understanding.

These assurances have been given to me from the highest level of the Soviet Government.

Although we have persuasive evidence that the unit has been a combat brigade, the Soviet statements about the future non-combat status of the unit are significant.

However, we shall not rest on these Soviet statements alone. First, we will monitor the status of the Soviet forces by increased surveillance of Cuba. Second, we will assure that no Soviet unit in Cuba can be used as a combat force to threaten the security of the United States or any other nation in this hemisphere.

Those nations can be confident that the United States will act in response to a request for assistance to meet any such threat from Soviet or Cuban forces.

This policy is consistent with our responsibilities as a member of the Organization of American States and a party to the Rio Treaty. It is a reaffirmation in new circumstances of John F. Kennedy's declaration in 1963 "that we would not permit any troops from Cuba to move off the Island of Cuba in an offensive action against any neighboring countries."

Third, I am establishing a permanent, full-time Caribbean joint task force headquarters at Key West, Florida. I will assign to this headquarters forces from all the military services responsible for expanded planning and for conducting exercises. This headquarters unit will employ designated forces for action if required. This will substantially improve our capability to monitor and to respond rapidly to any attempted military encroachment in this region.

Fourth, we will expand military maneuvers in the region. We will conduct these exercises regularly from now on. In accordance with existing treaties, the United States will, of course, keep our forces in Guantanamo.

Fifth, we will increase our economic assistance to alleviate the unmet economic and human needs in the Caribbean region and further to ensure the ability of troubled peoples to resist social turmoil and possible communist domination.

The United States has a worldwide interest in peace and stability. Accordingly, I have directed the Secretary of Defense to further enhance the capacity of our rapid deployment forces to protect our own interests and to act in response to requests for help from our allies and friends. We must be able to move our ground, sea and air units to distant areas—rapidly and with adequate supplies.

We have reinforced our naval presence in the Indian Ocean.

We are enhancing our intelligence capability in order to monitor Soviet and Cuban military activities—both in Cuba and throughout the world. We will increase our efforts to guard against damage to our crucial intelligence sources and our methods of collection, without imparing civil and constitutional rights.

These steps reflect my determination to preserve peace, to strengthen our alliances, and to defend the interests of the United States. In developing them, I have consulted not only with my own advisers, but with Congressional leaders and with a bipartisan group of distinguished American citizens as well. The decisions are my own, and I take full responsibility for them as President and as Commander-in-Chief.

I have concluded that the brigade issue is certainly no reason for a return to the Cold War. A confrontation might be emotionally satisfying for a few days or weeks for some people, but it would be destructive to the national interest and to the security of the United States.

We must continue the basic policy that the United States has followed for 20 years, under six Administrations of both parties—a policy that recognizes that we are in competition with the Soviet Union in some fields and that we seek cooperation in others—notably maintaining the peace and controlling nuclear arms.

My fellow Americans, the greatest danger to American security tonight is certainly not the two or three thousand Soviet troops in Cuba. The greatest danger to all the nations of the world—including the United States and the Soviet Union—is the breakdown of a common effort to preserve the peace, and the ultimate threat of a nuclear war.

I renew my call to the Senate of the United States to ratify the SALT II Treaty.

SALT II is a solid treaty. Ensuring compliance with its terms will not be a matter of trust. We have highly sophisticated national technical means, carefully focused on the Soviet Union to ensure that the treaty is verifiable. This treaty is the most important step ever taken to control strategic nuclear arms.

It permits us to strengthen our defense and to preserve the strategic balance at lower risk and lower cost. During the past few years we have made real increases in our defense expenditures to fulfill the goals of our five-year defense plan. With SALT II we can concentrate these increases in areas where our interests are most threatened and where direct military challenge is most likely.

The rejection of SALT would seriously compromise our Nation's peace and security.

Of course we have disagreements with the Soviets. Of course we have conflicts with them. If we did not have these disagreements and conflicts, we would not need a treaty to reduce the possibility of nuclear war between us.

If SALT II is rejected, these disagreements and conflicts could take on a new and ominous dimension. Against the background of an uncontrolled nuclear arms race, every confrontation or dispute would carry the seeds of a nuclear confrontation.

In addition, SALT II is crucial to American leadership and to the further strengthening of the Western Alliance. Obviously a secure Europe is vital to our own security.

The leaders of our European allies support SALT II—unanimously. We have talked to a number of those leaders in the last few days. I must tell you tonight that if the Senate fails to approve the SALT Treaty, these leaders and their countries would be confused and deeply alarmed. If our allies should lose confidence in our ability to negotiate successfully for the control of nuclear weapons, then our effort to build a stronger and more united NATO could fail.

I know that for Members of Congress this is a troubling and difficult issue in a troubling and difficult time. But the Senate has a tradition of being the greatest deliberative body in the world, and the whole world is watching the Senate today. I am confident that all Senators will perform their high responsibilities as the national interest requires.

Politics and nuclear arsenals do not mix.

We must not play politics with the security of the United States. We must not play politics with the survival of the human race. We must not play politics with SALT II. It is much too important for that—too vital to our country, to our allies, and to the cause of peace.

The purpose of the SALT II Treaty and the purpose of my actions in dealing with Soviet and Cuban military relationships are exactly the same—to keep our Nation secure and to maintain a world at peace.

As a powerful nation—as a superpower—we have special responsibilities to maintain stability even when there are serious disagreements among nations.

We have had fundamental differences with the Soviet Union since 1917. I have no illusions about these differences. The best way to deal with them successfully is to maintain American unity, American will, and American strength.

That is what I am determined to do.

The struggle for peace—the long, hard struggle to bring weapons of mass destruction under control of human reason and human law—is a central drama of our age.

At another time of challenge in our Nation's history, President Abraham Lincoln told the American people: "We shall nobly save, or meanly lose, the last best hope of earth."

We acted wisely then, and preserved the Nation. Let us act wisely now, and preserve the world.

APPENDIX F

Background on the Question of the
Soviet Troops in Cuba
Department of State Press Release
October 1, 1979

Following is background information on the question of Soviet troops in Cuba, with questions and answers on some of the specific points raised during briefings held prior to the President's broadcast to the nation, October 1, 1979.

The surveillance of Cuba which was being conducted at the time of the 1962 Cuban missile crisis noted the existence of Soviet ground combat units deployed at four major locations and at several sublocations. One of the major locations was the same as one at which major elements of the combat unit now in question have been located.

In the course of the negotiations that took place in 1963, the U.S. called to the attention of the Soviets the fact that these ground combat units were present. Out of those discussions came a commitment on the part of Chairman Krushchev, made to President Kennedy, that he would ship out of Cuba the ground combat units which had anything to do with guarding the Soviet missile installations and bomber bases.

In 1963 the United States Government conducted extensive surveillance and checked, among other things, whether or not the ground combat units were being removed.

By 1964 the U.S. intelligence community had concluded that the Soviet ground combat units had been essentially withdrawn from Cuba.

At the same time there can be no question that there was a substantial Soviet military presence in Cuba in 1962 and that there has been a continuous military presence since then.

There is also no question that the Soviet military presence changed its mission in '63–'64 from being there to maintain missiles, to something else.

It is clear today that in the post-missile crisis period the Soviet forces in Cuba did not have enough equipment, or enough facilities, and did not conduct enough training activity, to be the kind of a combat unit that we see there today. In short, the mission and the structure of this brigade has changed at least once more since the change after the post-missile-crisis in 1962.

When precisely it reached its present form is unclear to us today, but there is a high degree of confidence that it is not a unit with a primary purpose of training Cubans. The observed pattern of activity of this unit over the past several years does not include any substantial involvement with the training of Cubans or Cuban ground forces. It does not show any pattern of interplay between Soviet forces and personnel, and Cuban forces and people.

The pattern of activity that can be seen is definitely similar to the patterns of activity of ground combat units inside the Soviet Union, carrying out their normal combat training.

The organization of this unit, its facilities and its equipment, are not those which would logically be there if it were going to perform a function of training other people. The organization, the facilities, the equipment are those which can be seen in Soviet units of this type inside the Soviet Union.

Soviets in military advisory capacities elsewhere in the world have not performed in this kind of a pattern with this kind of an organization, with these kinds of facilities and these amounts of equipment.

The conclusion can be drawn—after looking at its organization, at its facilities, at its equipment, at its personnel and at its training activities—that it is not a brigade for training Cubans but that it is a brigade with a combat capability. This can be done through thorough intelligence research involving not simply detecting whether a Soviet military unit exists in Cuba but assessing the purpose of a known Soviet military presence in Cuba, its intentions, and its plans.

It can be said with confidence that the composition of the Soviet unit is known: it is a brigade; its organization is known: its rank structure, that it has three infantry and one tank battalions and that it is commanded by a Soviet Army Colonel; its location is known: that it is garrisoned in two sites; its size is known: that it has about 2,600 people; its equipment is known: that it has 40 tanks, 60 armored personnel carriers and various other pieces of hardware; its training pattern is known: that that is similar to combat units in the Soviet Union; and it is known that it has no observable connections with the Cuban military.

Over a period of about three weeks negotiations have been conducted with the Soviets.

The Secretary of State has had six negotiating sessions with Soviet Ambassador Dobrynin, two with Foreign Minister Gromyko, and in addition to that there has been an exchange between the two heads of government.

The negotiating sessions with Dobrynin have lasted for considerable periods of time. In addition to these, there have been numerous telephone conversations.

The two sessions with the Foreign Minister in New York were reasonably lengthy and exhaustive.

The serious concern of the United States about the presence of this unit was made very clear to the Soviets in all these discussions. At the end of the negotiations the Soviets made certain statements, or assurances, which they have given to the United States:

Number one: That the unit in question is a training center; that it does nothing more than training, and can do nothing more.

Second, that they will not change its function or status as a training center. We understand this to mean that they do not intend to enlarge the unit or to give it additional capabilities.

Thirdly, that the Soviet personnel in Cuba are not and will not be a threat to the U.S. or to any other nation.

Fourthly, that they reaffirm the 1962 understanding and the mutually agreed confirmation of that understanding in 1970—and that they will abide by it in the future.

The United States, for its part, reconfirmed this understanding.

The assurances have been given to the President by the highest levels of the Soviet Government.

As indicated by the President, although there is persuasive evidence that the unit is a combat brigade, the Soviet statements about the future non-combat status of the unit are significant.

Again as the President points out, however, the United States will not rest on the Soviet statements alone, but will take a number of steps.

First, the U.S. will monitor the status of the Soviet forces by increasing surveillance of Cuba.

Second, the U.S. will assure that no Soviet unit in Cuba can be used as a combat force to threaten the security of the U.S. or any other nation in the hemisphere.

Third, the President is establishing a permanent, full time Caribbean Task Force Headquarters in Key West.

Fourth, the U.S. will expand military maneuvers in the region and conduct them regularly from now on.

The President also underscores that in accordance with existing treaty rights, the United States will, of course, keep its forces in Guantanamo.

Fifth, the U.S. will increase its economic assistance to alleviate the economic and human needs in the region. A supplemental appropriation bill will be submitted to the Congress in the very near future.

Next, the President has pointed out that the United States has a world-wide interest in peace and stability and that accordingly, he has directed further enhancement of the capacity of the Rapid Deployment Force to protect the interests of the U.S. and of its friends and allies.

The President further noted that the U.S. has already reinforced its naval presence in the Indian Ocean and is enhancing its intelligence capability in order to monitor Soviet and Cuban military activities both in Cuba and throughout the world. These steps reflect, as the President said, the determination of the U.S. to preserve peace, to strengthen the alliance, and to defend the interests of the United States.

The President's speech also stressed:

First, the very clear conclusion that the main issue is no reason to return to the cold war.

Secondly, that the basic policy of the United States for twenty years under six Administrations will be continued. This policy recognizes that while the U.S. is in competition with the Soviet Union it also seeks to cooperate in other areas—notably in maintaining peace and in controlling nuclear arms.

The President very clearly called upon the Congress to complete the work which is necessary for ratification of the SALT Treaty and to proceed with the debate on that treaty.

The President said it is of critical importance to us and to world peace—and to the security and well being of our allies—that this must go forward.

Q: Was the Soviet Union asked to remove the forces?

A: A number of suggestions and proposals for resolving this matter were sent forward by the U.S. Suggestions were made by the other side as well. At the end of those discussions, the assurances, statements, clarifications laid out very clearly in the President's statement were advanced.

Q: Reference was made to the evidence based on the facilities, the equipment, the organization, and the training pattern. The President said, "The Soviet statements about the future noncombat status of the unit are significant." Does that suggest that the Soviets have given any indication whatsoever that they will change either the facilities, the equipment, the organization, or the training?

A: Looking at the language itself, it says, for example, "The unit in question is a training center, and can do nothing more." It further says that "The status and the function will not be changed," and by that they mean not to enlarge the unit or give it additional capabilities. One of the additional capabilities which, obviously, the unit does not have now but would be significant is any airlift or sealift. They have said that they do not intend to enlarge the unit or give it additional capabilities.

Q: Combat status can be both offensive and defensive. Does it appear that the mission of these troops is perhaps to guard an installation that is important to the Soviets, perhaps a monitoring installation or an installation attempting to plug into our undersea grid?

A: The Soviets have a large monitoring facility in Cuba and it certainly can't be ruled out that one of the functions of this unit would be to protect it.

Q: Is there a difference in the way we view a brigade that has tanks and APCs that are there in sort of a "defensive" posture to guard a facility—and one that we would think is there in an offensive posture?

A: First, the size of the brigade and its equipment are inordinate to a function of protecting the intelligence-collection facility that the Soviets maintain in Cuba.

Secondly, the key question is whether or not it has a combat capability which can be projected in a way which constitutes a threat to the United States or others in the region.

Q: How has the status quo which was earlier said to be unacceptable been changed?

A: It has been changed in two ways:

First, very clearly, the President has outlined a number of steps that are going to be taken because it is felt they are necessary to protect U.S. national interests and those of our friends and allies.

Secondly, the Soviets have made certain statements. Those statements are believed to be significant insofar as they relate to the future. So from taking a look at those two sets of factors it can be seen that the status quo has been altered.

Q: Why should we take assurances about the future seriously when assurances about the past role of this brigade are not taken seriously?

A: By observing and monitoring, by increasing collection activities, by what is being done; at the same time by taking additional steps to strengthen our capabilities and to assure that we have the capability to protect ourselves and our neighbors in the hemisphere from any threat to them or to their security.

Q: Is it really possible, politically, in the real world, to separate this sequence of events from what is going on in the Senate with the SALT Treaty?

A: The Senators obviously will be reading very carefully what the President has to say tonight. We believe very deeply that SALT should be judged on its own merits. A great many of the Senators who are concerned about this issue, however, are also very concerned about SALT—and feel that it should go forward on its own merits.

And indeed, even in situations of tension like this, such as we have had, it is all the more important to have agreement on such fundamental matters as strategic balance, or factors that affect our two nations.

Q: Does this training facility, or combat headquarters, or whatever it is called, constitute a base in the sense that the president used that word?

A: We have not come to the conclusion that this constitutes a "base." We will continue to review the matter, but we have not come to that conclusion.

Q: How has this "incident" affected our overall relationship with the Soviets?

A: Both the Soviets and the U.S. have recognized very clearly that this matter, if not satisfactorily resolved, can have a serious effect on the relationship between our two countries and therefore, it has been a matter of serious concern to both of our nations.

That is why so much time has been given to this, at the highest level, starting with those at the head of government, the Foreign Ministers, and others. Obviously, this is a matter which both countries feel to be of great importance to our basic relationship.

Q: Would you say that its resolution has moved us forward, or set us back, or are we on an even plane?

A: It remains to be seen.

Q: The President referred to assurances from the "Soviets' highest level." Are we to assume, then, that this is the text of a message that Brezhnev sent to Mr. Carter?

A: You should make the assumption that what has been said precisely reflects statements that were made to us at the highest levels.

Q: Is this the language the Soviets used, or is this our summary, or interpretation of the language they used?

A: This is language which they used.

Q: Give us your perspective on this issue: How long has this brigade been there?

Is it a question of earlier administrations—earlier watches not picking up on this brigade down there. Deliberately ignoring it? Putting our resources elsewhere? Or did we just put it together here as of August 17 for a variety of reasons?

A: We cannot tell when it took this form and assumed this mission. It was at least three years ago—maybe somewhat longer.

This is not a condemnation of any previous administration.

In Cuba there are lots of tanks and APCs exactly like those in the Soviet unit. What we are trying to find out is, what has been the purpose for having this particular set of soldiers and equipment there. That is not easy and we are pleased that we were able, eventually, to put all these pieces together.

Q: Was it our assumption or expectation that in due course that unit would have been given sealift and airlift capability?

A: We have no evidence of any intent to do that.

Q: If we don't know what their mission is and how long they have been equipped and what they are doing, how can one say they are no threat to us?

A: We do know what they're doing. We know the kind of training they are doing; we know the kind of organization it is there. We don't know why the Soviet Union has decided that this is an appropriate unit for it to have in Cuba.

A brigade of Soviet forces is not a threat to the United States. We have available for use to defend ourselves, forces which to this are as a giant to an ant. We can deploy forces in the region that could swamp any such force. It is, therefore, not a threat in those terms to the United States. Nevertheless, as the President makes plain in his speech, the Soviet brigade is, and should be, a matter of some concern to the surrounding nations, and therefore, is to us too, because it might be used. The Cuban forces, which in Cuba amount to a much larger force than this Soviet brigade, could also be a threat if they were used to intervene in surrounding areas.

The actions that we are taking are not designed to greatly increase U.S. strength. U.S. strength and capability in this area already are very large. Our actions do serve to remind people that the problem is not of a magnitude that could threaten us. We have and will train and exercise forces which are very much larger than this, and could, should the contingency arise, take care of any such situation.

Q: Are you saying this "beefing up" is essentially political rather than military?

A: No. There are two pieces, you will recall. One is the establishment of a joint task force headquarters at Key West whose purpose will be to concentrate on planning and on training and on exercises, and as needed, on tactical surveillance, and should the need arise, conducting contingency operations.

Q: Will you reactivate the Key West Naval Station at Boca Chica?

A: The Key West Naval Station continues to exist. This is only a headquarters organization. It will be perhaps 60 to 100 people. We will, as necessary, assign to it forces for the functions that have been mentioned; that serves a very useful purpose in reminding us of our strength. Should it be necessary, it would conduct whatever operations are necessary.

Q: Are you going to go back and do the aerial reconnaissance of Cuba which was suspended in 1977?

A: The President's statement includes the statement that we will augment our surveillance as necessary; to the degree that it is necessary to use such assets, we will.

Q: If there is no real threat, then why must any additional action be taken? And what could they be setting out to prevent?

A: There is not a threat to the immediate security of the United States. This force and the overall Soviet-Cuban military relationship, however, raise real questions and concerns in the minds of other countries in the region.

Q: Senator Church said several weeks ago that as long as the brigade as a combat brigade remained in Cuba, he saw no likelihood that the Senate would ratify SALT. Well, the brigade is going to remain apparently, so what assurance do you have now that SALT can be saved?

A: In talking to a number of Senators who have been briefed about the speech, in almost every case, the response that we have received is, "We believe that the SALT treaty hearings should go forward; we believe that it should be taken up on its own merits and we are prepared to do that." It is our best judgment that that will be the case.

Q: Could you describe the size of this Task Force that is going to be down there?

A: What we are establishing is a Task Force headquarters which will have perhaps 60 people, to begin with. It might expand to 100. It will be established beginning this week. It will have assigned to the headquarters personnel from Army, Navy, Air Force, and Marines, and it will, depending upon the particular things that it happens to be supervising at a particular time, have assigned to it operational forces from each of these services. And that might go anywhere from a battalion of Marines for some functions to a substantial Naval task force plus some air squadrons in others.

APPENDIX G

Letter from President Carter to Senator Stone January 27, 1978

THE WHITE HOUSE

WASHINGTON

January 27, 1978

To Senator Richard Stone

Thank you for meeting with me yesterday about the Panama Canal Treaties. You have expressed concerns that are shared by many of our citizens in Florida and throughout the nation.

Ratification of the Panama Canal Treaties should not be viewed by any power as signaling a retreat by the United States in Latin America. Our country will continue to play a visible and dynamic role in Western Hemisphere affairs.

In particular, it has been and will continue to be the policy of the United States to oppose any efforts, direct or indirect, by the Soviet Union to establish military bases in the Western Hemisphere. Moreover, we will maintain our military bases in the Caribbean necessary to the defense of the Panama Canal and the security of the United States and its allies in the Western Hemisphere.

You have asked when the Government of Panama plans to hold Assembly elections. I am pleased to inform you that Panama will hold elections for its National Assembly on August 6 of this year. The newly-elected members will take office in October.

You have done much to clarify ambiguities that have developed during the debate on the Panama Canal Treaties. I believe the Treaties are very important to the continuing improvement in our relations with Latin America and I hope they will have your support.

Sincerely,

Jimmy Carter
[signature]

The Honorable Richard Stone
United States Senate
Washington, D.C. 20510

APPENDIX H

Letter from Secretary Vance
to Senator Stone
July 27, 1979

THE SECRETARY OF STATE

WASHINGTON

July 27, 1979

Dear Senator Stone:

The President has asked me to respond to your July 24 letter to him on Soviet military presence in Cuba. I very much appreciate your calling to our attention reports of a possible high ranking Soviet command structure in Cuba.

I wish to reaffirm the President's statement to you that it is the policy of the United States to oppose any efforts, direct or indirect, by the Soviet Union to establish military bases in the Western Hemisphere. However, there is no evidence of any substantial increase of the Soviet military presence in Cuba over the past several years or of the presence of a Soviet military base. Apart from a military group that has been advising the Cuban Armed Forces for fifteen years or more our intelligence does not warrant the conclusion that there are any other significant Soviet forces in Cuba. At the same time the President directed that we give increased attention to the situation and monitor it closely. This is being done. The President raised the question of the Soviet presence in Cuba with President Brezhnev in Vienna and made clear to him that a Soviet buildup would adversely affect our relationship.

You have also raised questions on the 1962 understanding in your letter to the President and during the appearances of Secretary Brown and myself before the SFRC. The United States and the Soviet Union both recognize that an understanding on Cuba exists. This understanding is reflected in the Kennedy-Khrushchev correspondence of October and November, 1962, (particularly the letters of October 27 and 28, 1962) and in communications between the two governments in the Fall of 1970 concerning the establishment of Soviet naval bases in Cuba. We have no evidence that the Soviets are in violation of this understanding.

President Nixon addressed the scope of the understanding in 1971, and stated, "in the event that nuclear submarines were serviced either in Cuba or from Cuba, that would be a violation of the understanding. Subsequently, in the early 1970's, submarines did make occasional port calls. According to the understanding with the Soviet Union such port calls do not constitute violations.

You have asked that we assure the American people that they have full knowledge of the understanding. The essential understanding is in the public record. The Soviets agreed in 1962 that offensive weapons could not again be introduced into Cuba. In 1970 it was made clear that this understanding included sea-based systems.

Although the October 27 and 28, 1962, letters and many other documents from this period are not classified, there are additional diplomatic exchanges, made in confidence, which must remain classified. They are consistent with publicly available documents. The principle of confidentiality of diplomatic communication is respected throughout the international community and is carefully applied in our relations with the Soviet Union to ensure the free flow of communication that is essential to the maintenance of world peace. A breach of confidentiality in this context could easily impair our ability to deal with the Soviets in the future.

If you wish any further background, please do not hesitate to inform me.

With best wishes,

Sincerely,

Cyrus Vance
[signature]

Clearance   L – LStorch   PM – RBartholomew
            NSC – DAaron   WH – LCutler
            S/S – PTarnoff

A P P E N D I X   I

Statements by President Kennedy
September 4 and 13, 1962
and January 24, 1963

U.S. Reaffirms Policy on Prevention of Aggressive Actions by Cuba

Statement by President Kennedy[1]

All Americans, as well as all of our friends in this hemisphere, have been concerned over the recent moves of the Soviet Union to bolster the military power of the Castro regime in Cuba. Information has reached this Government in the last 4 days from a variety of sources which establishes without doubt that the Soviets have provided the Cuban Government with a number of antiaircraft defense missiles with a slant range of 25 miles which are similar to early models of our Nike. Along with these missiles, the Soviets are apparently providing the extensive radar and other electronic equipment which is required for their operation. We can also confirm the presence of several Soviet-made motor torpedo boats carrying ship-to-ship guided missiles having a range of 15 miles. The number of Soviet military technicians now known to be in Cuba or en route—approximately 3,500—is consistent with assistance in setting up and learning to use this equipment. As I stated last week, we shall continue to make information available as fast as it is obtained and properly verified.

There is no evidence of any organized combat force in Cuba from any Soviet bloc country; of military bases provided to Russia; of a violation of the 1934 treaty relating to Guantanamo; of the presence of offensive ground-to-ground missiles; or of other significant offensive capability either in Cuban hands or under Soviet direction and guidance. Were it to be otherwise, the gravest issues would arise.

The Cuban question must be considered as a part of the worldwide challenge posed by Communist threats to the peace. It must be dealt with as a part of that larger issue as well as in the context of the special relationships which have long characterized the inter-American system.

It continues to be the policy of the United States that the Castro regime will not be allowed to export its aggressive purposes by force or the threat of force. It will be prevented by whatever means may be necessary from taking action

Source: Department of State Bulletin, September 24, 1962, p. 450

against any part of the Western Hemisphere. The United States, in conjunction with other hemisphere countries, will make sure that while increased Cuban armaments will be a heavy burden to the unhappy people of Cuba themselves, they will be nothing more.

NOTE
1. Read to news correspondents on Sept. 4 by Pierre Salinger, White House Press Secretary.

**President States U.S. Policy
Toward Cuba**

Statement by President Kennedy[1]
There has been a great deal of talk on the situation in Cuba in recent days both in the Communist camp and in our own, and I would like to take this opportunity to set the matter in perspective.

In the first place it is Mr. Castro and his supporters who are in trouble. In the last year his regime has been increasingly isolated from this hemisphere. His name no longer inspires the same fear or following in other Latin American countries. He has been condemned by the OAS [Organization of American States],[2] excluded from the Inter-American Defense Board,[3] and kept out of the [Latin American] Free Trade Association. By his own monumental economic mismanagement, supplemented by our refusal to trade with him,[4] his economy has crumbled and his pledges for economic progress have been discarded, along with his pledges for political freedom. His industries are stagnating, his harvests are declining, his own followers are beginning to see that their revolution has been betrayed.

So it is not surprising that in a frantic effort to bolster his regime he should try to arouse the Cuban people by charges of an imminent American invasion and commit himself still further to a Soviet takeover in the hope of preventing his own collapse.

Ever since communism moved into Cuba in 1958, Soviet technical and military personnel have moved steadily onto the island in increasing numbers at the invitation of the Cuban government. Now that movement has been increased. It is under our most careful surveillance. But I will repeat the conclusion that I reported last week,[5] that these new shipments do not constitute a serious threat to any other part of this hemisphere.

If the United States ever should find it necessary to take military action against communism in Cuba, all of Castro's Communist-supplied weapons and technicians would not change the result or significantly extend the time required to achieve that result.

However, unilateral military intervention on the part of the United States cannot currently be either required or justified, and it is regrettable that loose talk about such action in this country might serve to give a thin color of legiti-

Source: Department of State Bulletin, October 1, 1962, pp.481–82

macy to the Communist pretense that such a threat exists. But let me make this clear once again: If at any time the Communist buildup in Cuba were to endanger or interfere with our security in any way, including our base at Guantanamo, our passage to the Panama Canal, our missile and space activities at Cape Canaveral, or the lives of American citizens in this country, or if Cuba should ever attempt to export its aggressive purposes by force or the threat of force against any nation in this hemisphere, or become an offensive military base of significant capacity for the Soviet Union, then this country will do whatever must be done to protect its own security and that of its allies.

We shall be alert to, and fully capable of dealing swiftly with, any such development. As President and Commander in Chief I have full authority now to take such action, and I have asked the Congress to authorize me to call up reserve forces should this or any other crisis make it necessary.

In the meantime we intend to do everything within our power to prevent such a threat from coming into existence. Our friends in Latin America must realize the consequences such developments hold out for their own peace and freedom, and we shall be making further proposals to them. Our friends in NATO must realize the implications of their ships' engaging in the Cuban trade.

We shall continue to work with Cuban refugee leaders who are dedicated as we are to that nation's future return to freedom. We shall continue to keep the American people and the Congress fully informed. We shall increase our surveillance of the whole Caribbean area. We shall neither initiate nor permit aggression in this hemisphere.

With this in mind, while I recognize that rash talk is cheap, particularly on the part of those who did not have the responsibility, I would hope that the future record will show that the only people talking about a war and invasion at this time are the Communist spokesmen in Moscow and Habana, and that the American people, defending as we do so much of the free world, will in this nuclear age, as they have in the past, keep both their nerve and their head.

NOTES

1. Read by the President at his news conference on September 13.
2. For background, see BULLETIN of February 19, 1962, pp. 267 and 270.
3. Ibid., p. 281.
4. Ibid., p. 283.
5. Ibid., September 24, 1962, p. 450.

**The President's News Conference of
January 24, 1963**

[4.] **Q.** Mr. President, there are new reports of a Soviet military buildup in Cuba. I wonder if there's any truth to this report and if it might pose a threat to our intelligence operation there, our surveillance.

THE PRESIDENT. No, we have been conducting continued surveillance. The best information we have is that one ship has arrived since the October crisis, which may have arms on it, and possibly military cargo. But there has not been a military buildup, in that sense, of equipment coming in from outside

Source: Department of State Bulletin, October 1, 1962, pp.481–82

of Cuba. There's no evidence that this ship carried any offensive weapons.

Now, on Cuba itself, there are still—we think that probably about 4,500 Soviet technicians who were connected with the offensive weapons were withdrawn after the late October agreement. We figure there are still approximately 16 or 17 thousand Russians there, that the Soviets are continuing to operate the SAM sites and other technical pieces of equipment, and there are some organized units, the same organized units we've described before, which are still on the territory of Cuba. They are exercising, building some barracks. That is the kind of activity which is going on. There is no influx of military equipment, other than the ship. And, as I say, our scrutiny of Cuba is daily.

Source: *Public Papers of the Presidents of the United States* (D.C.: U.S. Government Printing Office), pp. 93–94.

A P P E N D I X J

Khrushchev and Kennedy
Exchange of Messages
October 27–28, 1962

Chairman Khrushchev's Message
of October 27, 1962[1]

Informal Translation[2]

DEAR MR. PRESIDENT: It is with great satisfaction that I studied your reply to Mr. U Thant on the adoption of measures in order to avoid contact by our ships and thus avoid irreparable fatal consequences. This reasonable step on your part persuades me that you are showing solicitude for the preservation of peace, and I note this with satisfaction.

I have already said that the only concern of our people and government and myself personally as chairman of the Council of Ministers is to develop our country and have it hold a worthy place among all people of the world in economic competition, advance of culture and arts, and the rise in people's living standards. This is the loftiest and most necessary field for competition which will only benefit both the winner and loser, because this benefit is peace and an increase in the facilities by means of which man lives and obtains pleasure.

In your statement, you said that the main aim lies not only in reaching agreement and adopting measures to avert contact of our ships, and, consequently, a deepening of the crisis, which because of this contact can spark off the fire of military conflict after which any talks would be superfluous because other forces and other laws would begin to operate—the laws of war. I agree with you that this is only a first step. The main thing is to normalize and stabilize the situation in the world between states and between people.

I understand your concern for the security of the United States, Mr. President, because this is the first duty of the president. However, these questions are also uppermost in our minds. The same duties rest with me as chairman of the USSR Council of Ministers. You have been worried over our assisting Cuba with arms

Source: Department of State Bulletin, November 19, 1973, pp. 646–65

designed to strengthen its defensive potential—precisely defensive potential—because Cuba, no matter what weapons it had, could not compare with you since these are different dimensions, the more so given up-to-date means of extermination. Our purpose has been and is to help Cuba, and no one can challenge the humanity of our motives aimed at allowing Cuba to live peacefully and develop as its people desire.

You want to relieve your country from danger and this is understandable. However, Cuba also wants this. All countries want to relieve themselves from danger. But how can we, the Soviet Union and our government, assess your actions which, in effect, mean that you have surrounded the Soviet Union with military bases, surrounded our allies with military bases, set up military bases literally around our country, and stationed your rocket weapons at them? This is no secret. High-placed American officials demonstratively declare this. Your rockets are stationed in Britain and in Italy and point at us. Your rockets are stationed in Turkey.

You are worried over Cuba. You say that it worries you because it lies at a distance of 90 miles across the sea from the shores of the United States. However, Turkey lies next to us. Our sentinels are pacing up and down and watching each other. Do you believe that you have the right to demand security for your country and the removal of such weapons that you qualify as offensive, while not recognizing this right for us? You have stationed devastating rocket weapons, which you call offensive, in Turkey literally right next to us. How then does recognition of our equal military possibilities tally with such unequal relations between our great states? This does not tally at all.

It is good, Mr. President, that you agreed for our representatives to meet and begin talks, apparently with the participation of U.N. Acting Secretary General U Thant. Consequently, to some extent, he assumes the role of intermediary, and we believe that he can cope with the responsible mission if, of course, every side that is drawn into this conflict shows good will.

I think that one could rapidly eliminate the conflict and normalize the situation. Then people would heave a sigh of relief, considering that the statesmen who bear the responsibility have sober minds, an awareness of their responsibility, and an ability to solve complicated problems and not allow matters to slide to the disaster of war.

This is why I make this proposal: We agree to remove those weapons from Cuba which you regard as offensive weapons. We agree to do this and to state this commitment in the United Nations. Your representatives will make a statement to the effect that the United States, on its part, bearing in mind the anxiety and concern of the Soviet state, will evacuate its analogous weapons from Turkey. Let us reach an understanding on what time you and we need to put this into effect. After this, representatives of the U.N. Security Council could control on-the-spot the fulfillment of these commitments. Of course, it is necessary that the Governments of Cuba and Turkey would allow these representatives to come to their countries and check fulfillment of this commitment, which each side undertakes. Apparently, it would be better if these representatives enjoyed the trust of the Security Council and ours—the United States and the Soviet Union—as well as of Turkey and Cuba. I think that it will not be difficult to find such people who enjoy the trust and respect of all interested sides.

We, having assumed this commitment in order to give satisfaction and hope to the peoples of Cuba and Turkey and to increase their confidence in their security, will make a statement in the Security Council to the effect that the Soviet Government gives a solemn pledge to respect the integrity of the frontiers and the sovereignty of Turkey, not to intervene in its domestic affairs, not to invade Turkey, not to make available its territory as a place d'armes for such invasion, and also will restrain those who would think of launching an aggression against Turkey either from Soviet territory or from the territory of other states bordering on Turkey.

The U.S. Government will make the same statement in the Security Council with regard to Cuba. It will declare that the United States will respect the integrity of the frontiers of Cuba, its sovereignty, undertakes not to intervene in its domestic affairs, not to invade and not to make its territory available as place d'armes for the invasion of Cuba, and also will restrain those who would think of launching an aggression against Cuba either from U.S. territory or from the territory of other states bordering on Cuba.

Of course, for this we would have to reach agreement with you and to arrange for some deadline. Let us agree to give some time, but not to delay, two or three weeks, not more than a month.

The weapons on Cuba, that you have mentioned and which, as you say, alarm you, are in the hands of Soviet officers. Therefore any accidental use of them whatsoever to the detriment of the United States of America is excluded. These means are stationed in Cuba at the request of the Cuban Government and only in defensive aims. Therefore, if there is no invasion of Cuba, or an attack on the Soviet Union, or other of our allies then, of course, these means do not threaten anyone and will not threaten. For they do not pursue offensive aims.

If you accept my proposal, Mr. President, we would send our representatives to New York, to the United Nations, and would give them exhaustive instructions to order to come to terms sooner. If you would also appoint your men and give them appropriate instructions, this problem could be solved soon.

Why would I like to achieve this? Because the entire world is now agitated and expects reasonable actions from us. The greatest pleasure for all the peoples would be an announcement on our agreement, on nipping in the bud the conflict that has arisen. I attach a great importance to such understanding because it might be a good beginning and, specifically, facilitate a nuclear test ban agreement. The problem of tests could be solved simultaneously, not linking one with the other, because they are different problems. However, it is important to reach an understanding to both these problems in order to make a good gift to the people, to let them rejoice in the news that a nuclear test ban agreement has also been reached and thus there will be no further contamination of the atmosphere. Your and our positions on this issue are very close.

All this, possibly, would serve as a good impetus to searching for mutually acceptable agreements on other disputed issues, too, on which there is an exchange of opinion between us. These problems have not yet been solved but they wait for an urgent solution which would clear the international atmosphere. We are ready for this.

These are my proposals, Mr. President.

Respectfully yours,

NIKITA KHRUSHCHEV.

[MOSCOW,] *October 27, 1962.*

Official Translation[3]

DEAR MR. PRESIDENT, I have studied with great satisfaction your reply to Mr. Thant concerning measures that should be taken to avoid contact between our vessels and thereby avoid irreparable and fatal consequences. This reasonable step on your part strengthens my belief that you are showing concern for the preservation of peace, which I note with satisfaction.

I have already said that our people, our Government, and I personally, as Chairman of the Council of Ministers, are concerned solely with having our country develop and occupy a worthy place among all peoples of the world in economic competition, in the development of culture and the arts, and in raising the living standard of the people. This is the most noble and necessary field for competition, and both the victor and the vanquished will derive only benefit from it, because it means peace and an increase in the means by which man lives and finds enjoyment.

In your statement you expressed the opinion that the main aim was not simply to come to an agreement and take measures to prevent contact between our vessels and consequently a deepening of the crisis which could, as a result of such contacts, spark a military conflict, after which all negotiations would be superfluous because other forces and other laws would then come into play— the laws of war. I agree with you that this is only the first step. The main thing that must be done is to normalize and stabilize the state of peace among states and among peoples.

I understand your concern for the security of the United States, Mr. President, because this is the primary duty of a President. But we too are disturbed about these same questions; I bear these same obligations as Chairman of the Council of Ministers of the U.S.S.R. You have been alarmed by the fact that we have aided Cuba with weapons, in order to strengthen its defense capability—precisely defense capability—because whatever weapons it may possess, Cuba cannot be equated with you since the difference in magnitude is so great, particularly in view of modern means of destruction. Our aim has been and is to help Cuba, and no one can dispute the humanity of our motives, which are oriented toward enabling Cuba to live peacefully and develop in the way its people desire.

You wish to ensure the security of your country, and this is understandable. But Cuba, too, wants the same thing; all countries want to maintain their security. But how are we, the Soviet Union, our Government, to assess your actions which are expressed in the fact that you have surrounded the Soviet Union with military bases; surrounded our allies with military bases; placed military bases lieterally around our country; and stationed your missile armaments there? This is no secret. Responsible American personages openly declare that it is so. Your missiles are located in Britain, are located in Italy, and are aimed against us. Your missiles are located in Turkey.

You are disturbed over Cuba. You say that this disturbs you because it is 90 miles by sea from the coast of the United States of America. But Turkey adjoins us; our sentries patrol back and forth and see each other. Do you consider, then, that you have the right to demand security for your own country and the removal of the weapons you call offensive, but do not accord the same right to us? You have placed destructive missile weapons, which you call offensive, in Turkey, literally next to us. How then can recognition of our equal military capacities be reconciled with such unequal relations between our great states? This is irreconcilable.

It is good, Mr. President, that you have agreed to have our representatives meet and begin talks, apparently through the mediation of U Thant, Acting Secretary General of the United Nations. Consequently, he to some degree has assumed the role of a mediator and we consider that he will be able to cope with this responsible mission, provided, of course, that each party drawn into this controversy displays good will.

I think it would be possible to end the controversy quickly and normalize the situation, and then the people could breathe more easily, considering that statesmen charged with responsibility are of sober mind and have an awareness of their responsibility combined with the ability to solve complex questions and not bring things to a military catastrophe.

I therefore make this proposal: We are willing to remove from Cuba the means which you regard as offensive. We are willing to carry this out and to make this pledge in the United Nations. Your representatives will make a declaration to the effect that the United States, for its part, considering the uneasiness and anxiety of the Soviet State, will remove its analogous means from Turkey. Let us reach agreement as to the period of time needed by you and by us to bring this about. And, after that, persons entrusted by the United Nations Security Council could inspect on the spot the fulfillment of the pledges made. Of course, the permission of the Goverments of Cuba and of Turkey is necessary for the entry into those countries of these representatives and for the inspection of the fulfillment of the pledge made by each side. Of course it would be best if these representatives enjoyed the confidence of the Security Council, as well as yours and mine—both the United States and the Soviet Union—and also that of Turkey and Cuba. I do not think it would be difficult to select people who would enjoy the trust and respect of all parties concerned.

We, in making this pledge, in order to give satisfaction and hope of [to] the peoples of Cuba and Turkey and to strengthen their confidence in their security, will make a statement within the framework of the Security Council to the effect that the Soviet Government gives a solemn promise to respect the inviolability of the borders and sovereignty of Turkey, not to interfere in its internal affairs, not to invade Turkey, not to make available our territory as a bridgehead for such an invasion, and that it would also restrain those who contemplate committing aggression against Turkey, either from the territory of the Soviet Union or from the territory of Turkey's other neighboring states.

The United States Government will make a similar statement within the framework of the Security Council regarding Cuba. It will declare that the United States will respect the inviolability of Cuba's borders and its sovereignty, will pledge not to interfere in its internal affairs, not to invade Cuba itself or make its territory available as a bridgehead for such an invasion, and will also restrain those who might contemplate committing aggression against Cuba, either from the territory of the United States or from the territory of Cuba's other neighboring states.

Of course, for this we would have to come to an agreement with you and specify a certain time limit. Let us agree to some period of time, but without unnecessary delay—say within two or three weeks, not longer than a month.

The means situated in Cuba, of which you speak and which disturb you, as you have stated, are in the hands of Soviet officers. Therefore, any accidental use of them to the detriment of the United States is excluded. These means are situated in Cuba at the request of the Cuban Government and are only for defense purposes. Therefore, if there is no invasion of Cuba, or attack on the Soviet Union or any of our other allies, then of course these means are not and will not be a threat to anyone. For they are not for purposes of attack.

If you are agreeable to my proposal, Mr. President, then we would send our representatives to New York, to the United Nations, and would give them comprehensive instructions in order that an agreement may be reached more quickly. If you also select your people and give them the corresponding instructions, then this question can be quickly resolved.

Why would I like to do this? Because the whole world is now apprehensive and expects sensible actions of us. The greatest joy for all peoples would be the announcement of our agreement and of the eradication of the controversy that has arisen. I attach great importance to this agreement in so far as it could serve as a good beginning and could in particular make it easier to reach agreement on banning nuclear weapons tests. The question of the tests could be solved in parallel fashion, without connecting one with the other, because these are different issues. However, it is important that agreement be reached on both these issues so as to present humanity with a fine gift, and also to gladden it with the news that agreement has been reached on the cessation of nuclear tests and that consequently the atmosphere will no longer be poisoned. Our position and yours on this issue are very close together.

All of this could possibly serve as a good impetus toward the finding of mutually acceptable agreements on other controversial issues on which you and I have been exchanging views. These issues have so far not been resolved, but they are awaiting urgent solution, which would clear up the international atmosphere. We are prepared for this.

These are my proposals, Mr. President.

Respectfully yours,

N. KHRUSHCHEV.

[MOSCOW,] *October 27, 1962.*

**President Kennedy's Message
of October 27, 1962[4]**

[WASHINGTON,] *October 27, 1962.*

DEAR MR. CHAIRMAN: I have read your letter of October 26th with great care and welcomed the statement of your desire to seek a prompt solution to the problem. The first thing that needs to be done, however, is for work to cease on offensive missile bases in Cuba and for all weapons systems in Cuba capable of offensive use to be rendered inoperable, under effective United Nations arrangements.

Assuming this is done promptly, I have given my representatives in New York instructions that will permit them to work out this weekend[5]—in cooperation with the Acting Secretary General and your representative—an arrangement for a permanent solution to the Cuban problem along the lines suggested in your letter of October 26th. As I read your letter, the key elements of your proposals—which seem generally acceptable as I understand them—are as follows:

1) You would agree to remove these weapons systems from Cuba under appropriate United Nations observation and supervision; and undertake, with suitable safeguards, to halt the further introduction of such weapons systems into Cuba.

2) We, on our part, would agree—upon the establishment of adequate arrangements through the United Nations to ensure the carrying out and continuation of these commitments—(a) to remove promptly the quarantine measures now in effect and (b) to give assurances against an invasion of Cuba.[6] I am confident that other nations of the Western Hemisphere would be prepared to do likewise.

If you will give your representative similar instructions, there is no reason why we should not be able to complete these arrangements and announce them to the world within a couple of days. The effect of such a settlement on easing world tensions would enable us to work toward a more general arrangement regarding "other armaments", as proposed in your second letter which you made public. I would like to say again that the United States is very much interested in reducing tensions and halting the arms race; and if your letter signifies that you are prepared to discuss a detente affecting NATO and the Warsaw Pact, we are quite prepared to consider with our allies any useful proposals.

But the first ingredient, let me emphasize, is the cessation of work on missile sites in Cuba and measures to render such weapons inoperable, under effective international guarantees. The continuation of this threat, or a prolonging of this discussion concerning Cuba by linking these problems to the broader questions of European and world security, would surely lead to an intensification of the Cuban crisis and a grave risk to the peace of the world. For this reason I hope we can quicky agree along the lines outlined in this letter and in your letter of October 26th.

JOHN F. KENNEDY.

Chairman Khrushchev's Message
of October 28, 1962[7]

Informal Translation[8]

DEAR MR. PRESIDENT: I have received your message of October 27. I express my satisfaction and thank you for the sense of proportion you have displayed and for realization of the responsibility which now devolves on you for the preservation of the peace of the world.

I regard with great understanding your concern and the concern of the United States people in connection with the fact that the weapons you describe as offensive are formidable weapons indeed.

Both you and we understand what kind of weapons these are.

In order to eliminate as rapidly as possible the conflict which endangers the cause of peace, to give an assurance to all people who crave peace, and to reassure the American people, who, I am certain, also want peace, as do the people of the Soviet Union, the Soviet Government, in addition to earlier instructions on the discontinuation of further work on weapons construction sites, has given a new order to dismantle the arms which you described as offensive, and to crate and return them to the Soviet Union.

Mr. President, I should like to repeat what I had already written to you in my earlier messages—that the Soviet Government has given economic assistance to the Republic of Cuba, as well as arms, because Cuba and the Cuban people were constantly under the continuous threat of an invasion of Cuba.

A piratic vessel had shelled Havana. They say that this shelling was done by irresponsible Cuban emigres. Perhaps so; however, the question is from where did they shoot. It is a fact that these Cubans have no territory, they are fugitives from their country, and they have no means to conduct military operations.

This means that someone put into their hands these weapons for shelling Havana and for piracy in the Caribbean in Cuban territorial waters. It is impossible in our time not to notice a piratic ship, considering the concentration in the Caribbean of American ships from which everything can be seen and observed. In these conditions, pirate ships freely roam around and shell Cuba and make piratic attacks on peaceful cargo ships. It is known that they even shelled a British cargo ship.

In a word, Cuba was under the continuous threat of aggressive forces, which did not conceal their intention to invade its territory.

The Cuban people want to build their life in their own interests without external interference. This is their right, and they cannot be blamed for wanting to be masters of their own country and disposing of the fruits of their own labor. The threat of invasion of Cuba and all other schemes for creating tension over Cuba are designed to strike the Cuban people with a sense of insecurity, intimidate them, and prevent them from peacefully building their new life.

Mr. President, I should like to say clearly once more that we could not remain indifferent to this. The Soviet Government decided to render assistance to Cuba with the means of defense against aggression—only with means for defense purposes. We have supplied the defense means which you describe as offensive means. We have supplied them to prevent an attack on Cuba—to prevent rash acts.

I regard with respect and trust the statement you made in your message of October 27, 1962, that there would be no attack, no invasion of Cuba, and not only on the part of the United States, but also on the part of other nations of the Western Hemisphere, as you said in your same message. Then the motives which induced us to render assistance of such a kind to Cuba disappear. It is for this reason that we instructed our officers—these means as I had already informed you earlier are in the hands of the Soviet officers—to take appropriate measures to discontinue construction of the aforementioned facilities, to dismantle them, and to return them to the Soviet Union. As I had informed you in the letter of October 27, we are prepared to reach agreement to enable United Nations Representatives to verify the dismantling of these means.

Thus in view of the assurances you have given and our instructions on dismantling, there is every condition for eliminating the present conflict.

I note with satisfaction that you have responded to the desire I expressed with regard to elimination of the aforementioned dangerous situation, as well as with regard to providing conditions for a more thoughtful appraisal of the international situation, fraught as it is with great dangers in our age of thermonuclear weapons, rocketry, spaceships, global rockets, and other deadly weapons. All people are interested in insuring peace.

Therefore, vested with trust and great responsibility, we must not allow the situation to become aggravated and must stamp out the centers where a dangerous situation fraught with grave consequences to the cause of peace has arisen. If we, together with you, and with the assistance of other people of good will, succeed in eliminating this tense atmosphere, we should also make certain that no other dangerous conflicts which could lead to a world nuclear catastrophe would arise.

In conclusion, I should like to say something about a detente between NATO and the Warsaw Treaty countries that you have mentioned. We have spoken about this long since and are prepared to continue to exchange views on this question with you and to find a reasonable solution. We should like to continue the exchange of views on the prohibition of atomic and thermonuclear weapons, general disarmament, and other problems relating to the relaxation of international tension.

Although I trust your statement, Mr. President, there are irresponsible people who would like to invade Cuba now and thus touch off a war. If we do take practical steps and proclaim the dismantling and evacuation of the means in question from Cuba, in so doing we, at the same time, want the Cuban people to be certain that we are with them and are not absolving ourselves of responsibility for rendering assistance to the Cuban people.

We are confident that the people of all countries, like you, Mr. President, will understand me correctly. We are not threatening. We want nothing but peace. Our country is now on the upsurge. Our people are enjoying the fruits of their peaceful labor. They have achieved tremendous successes since the October Revolution, and created the greatest material, spiritual, and cultural values. Our people are enjoying these values; they want to continue developing their achievements and insure their further development on the way of peace and social progress by their persistent labor.

I should like to remind you, Mr. President, that military reconnaissance planes have violated the borders of the Soviet Union. In connection with this there have been conflicts between us and notes exchanged. In 1960 we shot down your U–2 plane, whose reconnaissance flight over the USSR wrecked the summit meeting in Paris. At that time, you took a correct position and denounced that criminal act of the former U.S. Administration.

But during your term of office as President another violation of our border has occurred, by an American U–2 plane in the Sakhalin area. We wrote you about that violation on 30 August. At that time you replied that that violation had occurred as a result of poor weather, and gave assurances that this would not be repeated. We trusted your assurance, because the weather was indeed poor in that area at that time.

But had not your planes been ordered to fly about our territory, even poor weather could not have brought an American plane into our airspace. Hence, the conclusion that this is being done with the knowledge of the Pentagon, which tramples on international norms and violates the borders of other states.

A still more dangerous case occurred on 28 October, when one of your reconnaissance planes intruded over Soviet borders in the Chukotka Peninsula area in the north and flew over our territory. The question is, Mr. President: How should we regard this. What is this: A provocation? One of your planes violates our frontier during this anxious time we are both experiencing, when everything has been put into combat readiness. Is it not a fact that an intruding American plane could be easily taken for a nuclear bomber, which might push us to a fateful step? And all the more so since the U.S. Government and Pentagon long ago declared that you are maintaining a continuous nuclear bomber patrol. Therefore, you can imagine the responsibility you are assuming, especially now, when we are living through such anxious times.[9]

I should like to express the following wish; it concerns the Cuban people. You do not have diplomatic relations. But through my officers in Cuba, I have reports that American planes are making flights over Cuba.

We are interested that there should be no war in the world, and that the Cuban people should live in peace. And besides, Mr. President, it is no secret that we have our people in Cuba. Under such a treaty with the Cuban Government we have sent there officers, instructors, mostly plain people: specialists, agronomists, zootechnicians, irrigators, land reclamation specialists, plain workers, tractor drivers, and others. We are concerned about them.

I should like you to consider, Mr. President, that violation of Cuban airspace by American planes could also lead to dangerous consequences. And if you do not want this to happen, it would [be] better if no cause is given for a dangerous situation to arise.

We must be careful now and refrain from any steps which would not be useful to the defense of the states involved in the conflict, which could only cause irritation and even serve as a provocation for a fateful step. Therefore, we must display sanity, reason, and refrain from such steps.

We value peace perhaps even more than other peoples because we went through a terrible war with Hitler. But our people will not falter in the face of any test. Our people trust their Government, and we assure our people and world public opinion that the Soviet Government will not allow itself to be provoked. But if the provocateurs unleash a war, they will not evade responsibility and the grave consequences a war would bring upon them. But we are confident that reason will triumph, that war will not be unleashed and peace and the security of the peoples will be insured.

In connection with the current negotiations between Acting Secretary General U Thant and representatives of the Soviet Union, the United States, and the Republic of Cuba, the Soviet Government has sent First Deputy Foreign Minister V. V. Kuznetsov to New York to help U Thant in his noble efforts aimed at eliminating the present dangerous situation.

Respectfully yours,

N. KHRUSHCHEV.

[MOSCOW,] *October 28, 1962.*

Official Translation[10]

DEAR MR. PRESIDENT: I have received your message of October 27, 1962. I express my satisfaction and appreciation for the sense of proportion you have displayed, and for your understanding of the responsibility you now bear for the preservation of peace throughout the world.

I regard with great understanding your apprehension and the apprehension of the people of the United States of America over the fact that the weapons which you describe as offensive are indeed terrible weapons.

Both you and we understand what kind of weapons they are.

In order to eliminate as rapidly as possible a conflict which endangers the cause of peace, to give confidence to all peoples longing for peace, and to reassure the people of America, who, I am sure, want peace as much as the peoples of the Soviet Union, the Soviet Government, in addition to previously issued instructions for the cessation of further work at the weapons construction sites, has issued a new order to dismantle the weapons, which you describe as offensive, and to crate and return them to the Soviet Union.

Mr. President, I would like to repeat, as I have already stated in my previous letters, that the Soviet Government has extended economic aid as well as arms to the Government of Cuba, since Cuba and the Cuban people have constantly been under the continual threat of an invasion of Cuba.

A piratical vessel has shelled Havana. It is said that irresponsible Cuban émigrés did the shooting. This is possibly the case. But the question arises: from where did they shoot? After all, these Cubans have no territory; they are fugitives from their homeland; they have no funds for conducting military actions.

This means that someone put into their hands the weapons for shelling Havana and for piratical acts in the Caribbean, in Cuban territorial waters. It is unthinkable in our time that a pirate ship could pass unnoticed, particularly considering the saturation of the Caribbean with American ships from which literally all of this is seen and observed. And in such circumstances pirate ships freely roam about Cuba, shell Cuba, and carry out piratical attacks upon peaceful cargo ships. It is, after all, known that they even shelled a British freighter.

In short, Cuba has been under a continual threat from aggressive forces that have not concealed their intention to invade Cuba's territory.

The Cuban people wish to build their life in their own interests without external interference. This is their right, and they cannot be blamed for wanting to be masters of their own country and to enjoy the fruits of their labor. The threat of a Cuban invasion and all the other designs aimed at surrounding Cuba with tension are designed to engender uncertainty in the Cuban people, to intimidate them, and to hinder them in freely building their new life.

Mr. President, I want to say clearly once again that we could not be indifferent to this, and so the Soviet Government decided to help Cuba with means of defense against aggression—means only for purposes of defense. We placed means of defense there, means which you call offensive. We placed them there in order that no attack might be made against Cuba and that no rash acts might be permitted.

I regard with respect and trust the statement you made in your message of October 27, 1962, that no attack would be made on Cuba and that no invasion would take place—not only on the part of the United States, but also on the part of other countries of the Western Hemisphere, as your same message pointed out. In view of this, the motives which prompted us to give aid of this nature to Cuba no longer prevail. Hence, we have instructed our officers (these means, as I have already reported to you, are in the hands of Soviet officers) to take the necessary measures to stop the construction of the facilities indicated, and to dismantle and return them to the Soviet Union. As I have already informed you in my letter of October 27, we are prepared to come to an agreement with you to enable representatives of the U.N. to verify the dismantling of these means.

In this way, on the basis of the assurances you have made and of our orders to dismantle, there appear to exist all the necessary conditions for the elimination of the conflict which has arisen.

I note with satisfaction that you have echoed my desire that this dangerous situation be eliminated and also that conditions be created for a more thorough appraisal of the international situation, which is fraught with great dangers in our age of thermonuclear weapons, rocket technology, space ships, global rockets, and other lethal weapons. All mankind is interested in ensuring peace.

Therefore, we who bear great trust and responsibility must not permit the situation to become aggravated but must eliminate breeding grounds where dangerous situations are created, fraught with serious consequences for the cause of peace. And if we, together with you and other people of good will, succeed in eliminating this tense situation, we must also concern ourselves with seeing that other dangerous conflicts do not arise which might lead to a world thermonuclear catastrophe.

In conclusion, I should like to say something about the improvement of relations between NATO and the states of the Warsaw Pact, which you mention. We spoke of this a long time ago, and are ready to continue exchanging opinions with you on this question and to find a reasonable solution. We also wish to continue to exchange opinions on the prohibition of atomic and thermonuclear weapons, on general disarmament, and on other questions relating to relaxation of international tensions.

Mr. President, I place belief in your statement. On the other hand there are irresponsible people who would like to carry out an invasion of Cuba at this time and thereby unleash a war. If we take practical steps and announce the dismantling and evacuation of the above-mentioned means from Cuba, in doing so we at the same time want the Cuban people to be sure that we are with them and are not relieving ourselves of the responsibility of granting aid to the Cuban people.

We are convinced that the peoples of all countries will, like yourself, Mr. President, understand me correctly. We do not threaten. We desire only peace. Our country is now on the upswing. Our people are enjoying the fruits of their peaceful labor. They have achieved tremendous successes since the October Revolution, and have created the greatest material, spiritual, and cultural values. Our people are making use of these values and want to develop their achievements further and by their steadfast labor to ensure even greater growth along the path of peace and social progress.

I should like, Mr. President, to remind you that military aircraft of a reconnaissance nature have violated the frontiers of the Soviet Union—over which matter we had a controversy with you, and an exchange of notes took place. In 1960 we shot down your U–2 aircraft, whose reconnaissance flight over the U.S.S.R. led to the disruption of the summit meeting in Paris. You took a correct position at the time in condemning that criminal action on the part of the previous Administration of the United States.

But during your term of office as President, a second case of violation of our frontier by an American U–2 aircraft has taken place in the Sakhalin area. We informed you of this violation on August 30. You then replied that this violation had occurred as a result of bad weather and gave assurances that it would not be repeated. We accepted your assurances because there was, indeed, bad weather in that area at the time.

However, if your aircraft had not been given a mission to fly near our territory, then even bad weather could not have led an American aircraft into our air space. The conclusion follows that this is done with the knowledge of the Pentagon, which tramples on international norms and violates the frontiers of other states.

An even more dangerous case occurred on October 28, when your reconnaissance aircraft invaded the northern area of the Soviet Union, in the area of the Chukotski Peninsula, and flew over our territory. One asks, Mr. President, how we should regard this. What is this—a provocation? Your aircraft violates our frontier, and this happens at a time as troubled as the one through which we are now passing, when everything has been put in battle readiness. For an intruding U.S. aircraft can easily be taken for a bomber with nuclear weapons, and that can push us toward a fatal step. All the more so, because the U.S. Government and the Pentagon have long been saying that you continually maintain bombers with atomic bombs in the air. Therefore, you can imagine what kind of responsibility you assume, especially during such an anxious time as the present.

I should like to ask you to assess this correctly and to take steps accordingly, to prevent it from serving as a provocation to touch off a war.

I should also like to express to you the following wish. Of course, this is the Cuban people's affair—you do not at present maintain diplomatic relations, but through my officers in Cuba I have reports that American planes are conducting flights over Cuba.

We are interested in not having any war at all in the world and in the Cuban people's being able to live in peace. But, in addition to this, Mr. President, it is no secret that we have our people in Cuba. By agreement with the Cuban Government, we have there officers and instructors who are training the Cubans; they are mainly ordinary people, including specialists, agronomists, animal husbandry technicians, irrigation and reclamation experts, common laborers, tractor drivers, and others. We have concern for them.

I should like to ask you, Mr. President, to bear in mind that a violation of Cuban air space by American aircraft may also have dangerous consequences. And if you do not want that, no cause should be given for the creation of a dangerous situation.

We must now be very cautious and refrain from any acts that would not help in the defense of the states involved in the controversy, but which could arouse only irritation, and even prove to be a provocation for a fatal step. We must therefore display sense and wisdom, and refrain from acts of that kind.

We value peace, perhaps even more than other peoples, because we experienced a terrible war against Hitler. But our people will not flinch in the face of any ordeal; our people trust their own government, and we assure our own people and world public opinion that the Soviet Government will not allow itself to be provoked. But if the provocateurs unleash a war, they will not escape the responsibility and the grave consequences that war will bring to them. We are confident, however, that reason will prevail, that war will not be unleashed, and that the peace and security of peoples will be ensured.

In regard to the current negotiations of Acting Secretary General U Thant, with representatives of the Soviet Union, the United States of America and the Republic of Cuba, the Soviet Government has sent to New York V. V. Kuznetsov, First Deputy Minister of Foreign Affairs of the U.S.S.R., with a view to assisting Mr. Thant in his noble efforts aimed at eliminating the present dangerous situation.

Respectfully yours,

N. KHRUSHCHEV.

[MOSCOW,] *October 28, 1962.*

**President Kennedy's Message
of October 28, 1962**[11]

[WASHINGTON,] *October 28, 1962.*
DEAR MR. CHAIRMAN: I am replying at once to your broadcast message of October twenty-eight, even though the official text has not yet reached me,

because of the great importance I attach to moving forward promptly to the settlement of the Cuban crisis. I think that you and I, with our heavy responsibilities for the maintenance of peace, were aware that developments were approaching a point where events could have become unmanageable. So I welcome this message and consider it an important contribution to peace.

The distinguished efforts of Acting Secretary General U Thant have greatly facilitated both our tasks. I consider my letter to you of October twenty-seventh and your reply of today as firm undertakings on the part of both our governments which should be promptly carried out. I hope that the necessary measures can at once be taken through the United Nations, as your message says, so that the United States in turn will be able to remove[12] the quarantine measures now in effect. I have already made arrangements to report all these matters to the Organization of American States, whose members share a deep interest in a genuine peace in the Caribbean area.

You referred in your letter to a violation of your frontier by an American aircraft in the area of the Chukotsk Peninsula. I have learned that this plane, without arms or photographic equipment, was engaged in an air sampling mission in connection with your nuclear tests. Its course was direct from Eielson Air Force Base in Alaska to the North Pole and return. In turning south, the pilot made a serious navigational error which carried him over Soviet territory. He immediately made an emergency call on open radio for navigational assistance and was guided back to his home base by the most direct route. I regret this incident and will see to it that every precaution is taken to prevent recurrence.

Mr. Chairman, both of our countries have great unfinished tasks and I know that your people as well as those of the United States can ask for nothing better than to pursue them free from the fear of war. Modern science and technology have given us the possibility of making labor fruitful beyond anything that could have been dreamed of a few decades ago.

I agree with you that we must devote urgent attention to the problem of disarmament, as it relates to the whole world and also to critical areas. Perhaps now, as we step back from danger, we can together make real progress in this vital field. I think we should give priority to questions relating to the proliferation of nuclear weapons, on earth and in outer space, and to the great effort for a nuclear test ban. But we should also work hard to see if wider measures of disarmament can be agreed and put into operation at an early date. The United States government will be prepared to discuss these questions urgently, and in a constructive spirit, at Geneva or elsewhere.

JOHN F. KENNEDY.

NOTES
1. Broadcast over Moscow radio at 5 p.m. Moscow time, October 27, 1962; Russian text delivered to the American Embassy at Moscow at the same hour.
2. Reprinted with corrected paragraphing from BULLETIN of November 12, 1962, pp. 741–743.

3. Prepared subsequently by the Department of State.

4. Reprinted from BULLETIN of November 12, 1962, p. 743. This message was transmitted by the Department of State to the American Embassy at Moscow at 8:05 p.m. Washington time, October 27, 1962; delivered to the Soviet Foreign Ministry at 10:30 a.m. Moscow time, October 28. Text also delivered to the Soviet Embassy at Washington during the evening of October 27 and released to the press.

5. As transmitted to Moscow, this passage read "week and".

6. As transmitted to Moscow, this sentence was joined with the following sentence with the word "and".

7. Broadcast over Moscow radio at 5.p.m. Moscow time, October 28, 1962; Russian text delivered to the American Embassy at Moscow at 5:10 p.m. on the same date.

8. Text of a Moscow broadcast in English; reprinted with corrections from BULLETIN of November 12, 1962, pp. 743–745.

9. See the official translation below for a paragraph omitted here.

10. Prepared subsequently by the Department of State.

11. Reprinted from BULLETIN on Nov. 12, 1962, pp. 745–746. This message was transmitted by the Department of State to the American Embassy at Moscow at 5:03 p.m. Washington time, Oct. 28, 1962; delivered to the Soviet Foreign Ministry at 6:08 a.m. Moscow time, Oct. 29. Text also delivered to the Soviet Embassy at Washington on Oct. 28 and released to the press at 4:35 p.m. on that date.

12. As transmitted to Moscow, the text read "in turn can remove".

NOTES

Preface

1. Gloria Duffy, "Crisis Mangling and the Cuban Brigade," *International Security,* Summer 1983, Vol. 8, No. 1, pp. 67–87.

2. Gloria Duffy, "Crisis Prevention in Cuba," in *Managing U.S.-Soviet Rivalry,* Alexander L. George, ed. (Boulder, Col.: Westview Press, 1983), Chap. 12, pp. 285–318.

3. Raymond L. Garthoff, "The 1979 Pseudo-Crisis over the Soviet Brigade in Cuba," seen in manuscript.

4. Cyrus Vance, *Hard Choices* (New York: Simon and Schuster, 1983), pp. 358–364; Zbigniew Brzezinski, *Power and Principle* (New York: Farrar, Strauss, Giroux, 1983), pp. 344–353; Jimmy Carter, *Keeping Faith* (New York: Bantam, 1982), pp. 262–264.

5. Don Oberdorfer, "Cuban Crisis Mishandled," *Washington Post,* 16 October 1979, A14.

Chapter One: U.S. Diplomacy and Politics

6. The Monroe Doctrine was so prominent an aspect of the debate that Secretary Vance commissioned a study of the significance of the doctrine.

Chapter Three: Cuba—An Emotional Issue

7. For more on the NSC role, see Duffy, "Crisis Mangling" (op. cit., note 1), p. 71.

8. "Vance Will Explain Policy on Soviet Subs, Stone Says," *Miami Herald,* 8 August 1979, 10-A. See also Duffy, "Crisis Prevention" (op. cit., note 2), p. 288.

9. "How Senator Stone Switched on Panama Canal Issue," *Miami Herald,* 7 February 1978, 7-A.

10. For text of letter, see Appendix G.

11. *Miami Herald,* 7 February 1978 (op. cit., note 9).

12. "Stone Gets Pressure on Canal-Pact Vote," *Miami Herald,* 15 April 1978, 26-A.

13. "How Senator Stone Built His Russian-Troops Case," Miami Herald, 14 September 1979, 7-A.

14. See Senate Foreign Relations Committee hearings on SALT II, 17 July 1979, p. 179.

15. The quote is from the Church/Javits press release, using the words of Secretary Brown's response. Quoted in *Miami Herald,* 14 September 1979 (op. cit., note 13).

16. For text of Vance letter, see Appendix H.

17. *Miami Herald,* 14 September 1979 (op. cit., note 13).

18. "Narrow 68–32 Victory," *New York Times,* 19 April 1978, A1–A16.

19. "Castro, Church Break the Ice, Talk Business," *New York Times*, 11 August 1977, All.

20. "Frank Church: Hero or Villain, or a Politician," *New York Times*, 12 September 1979, A10. See also Duffy, "Crisis Prevention" (op. cit., note 2) p. 303.

Chapter Four: The Use and Misuse of Intelligence

21. "Senate Panel Calls a Hearing on Intelligence in Cuba," *New York Times*, 7 September 1979, A6.

22. "Data Long Implied Soviet Units in Cuba," *New York Times*, 6 September 1979, A7.

23. "Soviet Brigade, How the U.S. Traced It," *New York Times*, 13 September 1979, A16.

24. "The 'Brigada': An Unwelcome Sighting in Cuba," *Washington Post*, 9 September 1979, A1.

25. *New York Times*, 13 September 1979 (op. cit., note 23). See also Duffy, "Crisis Prevention (op. cit., note 2), pp. 299–300.

26. "Soviet Troops in Cuba Possible, Stone Says," *Miami Herald*, 18 July 1979, 2-A.

27. See Vance letter, Appendix H.

28. *New York Times*, 13 September 1979 (op. cit., note 23).

Chapter Five: U.S.-Soviet Understandings

29. For speculation on who may have leaked, see Duffy, "Crisis Mangling" (op. cit., note 1).

30. Department of State Bulletin, 19 November 1973, pp. 645–647. See Appendix J for full text.

31. R. L. Garthoff, "American Reaction to Soviet Aircraft in Cuba, 1962 and 1978," *Political Science Quarterly*, Vol. 95, No. 3, Fall 1980, p. 436.

32. For a more complete account of these events, see Duffy, "Crisis Prevention," pp. 287ff. (op. cit., note 2).

33. See Carter letter to Stone, 27 January 1978 (Appendix G).

34. "US: Cuba Isn't Cheating on Ban," *Miami Herald*, 11 August 1979, 15-A.

35. Soviet Naval Activities in Cuba, Hearings before Subcommittee on Latin American Affairs of the Committee on Foreign Affairs, House of Representatives, 92nd Congress, 1st Session, 28 September 1971, Part 2, p. 2.

36. Soviet Naval Activities in Cuba, Hearings before Subcommittee on Latin American Affairs of the Committee on Foreign Affairs, House of Representatives, 93rd Congress, Parts 4 and 5, 20–21 November 1974, p. 65.

37. Henry Kissinger, *White House Years* (Boston: Little, Brown, 1979), p. 624.

38. Hearings Subcommittee on Inter-American Affairs, Foreign Affairs Committee, House of Representatives, 91st Congress, 13 September, 13 October, 19 November, 24 November, 1970, p.2.

39. "Cuba's MIG 23's," *Washington Post*, 15 November 1978, A19.

40. Statement made by President Nixon on TV broadcast/interview with John Chancellor (NBC), Nancy Dickerson (PBS), Eric Sevareid (CBS), and Howard K. Smith (ABC), 4 January 1971, excerpts printed in White House press release 4 January 1971. The President said, "Now in the event that nuclear submarines were serviced either in Cuba or from Cuba, that would be a violation of the understanding. That has not happened yet. We are watching the situation closely."

41. *Washington Post*, 15 November 1978 (op. cit., note 39). See also Duffy, "Crisis Prevention" (op. cit., note 2), p. 296.

42. Weekly compilation of Presidential Documents, 4 December 1978.

Chapter Six: Informing Congress and the Soviets
43. See Memorandum on the Monroe Doctrine and Cuba, 18 September 1979, and Briefing Memorandum on OAS Actions Concerning Cuba, Department of State, 24 September 1979.
44. Department of State Daily Press Briefing, Friday, 31 August 1979.
45. The account of the conversation with Vasev is based on the author's recollection and notes made at the time.
46. The accounts of the conversations with members of Congress are based on the author's recollections and notes made at the time. See also Duffy, "Crisis Prevention" (op. cit., note 2), p. 304.
47. For the exchange between Hodding Carter and the press, see Appendix A.
48. Ibid.

Chapter Seven: Managing the Issue
49. For instance, John Scali, then ABC correspondent at the United Nations, was approached by the Soviets during the Cuban missile crisis and became a significant go-between in the resolution of that affair.
50. *Washington Post*, 16 October 1979 (op. cit., note 5).
51. Department of State Release #216. 5 September 1979 (Appendix B).
52. *New York Times*, 7 September 1979 (op. cit., note 21). *Washington Post*, 9 September 1979 (op. cit., note 24).
53. "Church Delays Arms Pact Hearings to Study Soviet Troop Use in Cuba," *New York Times*, 5 September 1979, A1.
54. "Soviet Troop Talks Continue Amid a Swirl of Controversy," *Washington Post*, 12 September 1979, A9.
55. "Soviet Says Troops Are to Advise Cuba; Denies Combat Role," *New York Times*, 11 September 1979, A9.
56. "Kremlin Clouds Talks on Cuba," *Washington Star*, 11 September 1979, A1.
57. Presidential statement, 7 September 1979; see Appendix D.
58. "Talks Planned on Soviet Unit," *Washington Post*, 8 September 1979, A1. See Appendix C for text of Brzezinski's remarks.
59. "To Save SALT, Byrd Huddles Secretly with Dobrynin," *Washington Post*, 28 October 1979.
60. For a good analysis of the Soviet preception of these events, see Duffy, "Crisis Mangling" (op. cit., note 1), pp. 80–81, and "Crisis Prevention" (op. cit., note 2), p. 306.
61. As quoted in "Kremlin Defends Troops in Cuba," *Washington Post*, 11 September 1979, A1–A4.
62. *Washington Post*, 16 October 1979 (op. cit., note 5).
63. "U.S. Weighing View That Soviet Force Is Training Cubans," *New York Times*, 13 September 1979, A1–A7, and "U.S. Probes Soviet Unit's Role in Cuba," *Washington Post*, 13 September 1979, A1–A17.
64. "Jackson Says U.S. Seeks Deal with Soviets on Cuba," *New York Times*, 14 September 1979, A11.
65. "Gromyko Delivers Kremlin's Reply," *Washington Post*, 25 September 1979, A6.
66. "Carter Meets with Top Advisors," *Washington Post*, 18 September 1979, A10.
67. "Vance, Gromyko End Cuba Talks," *Washington Post*, 28 September 1979, A16.
68. "Brzezinski Cautions Soviets on Cuba Unit," *New York Times*, 23 September 1979, A1–A4.
69. "Hard or Soft on Cuba?" *Washington Post*, 24 September 1979, A23.

70. "A Small Soviet Brigade and Large Implications," *Washington Post*, 23 September 1979, A2.

71. The "Elder Statesmen" included Clark Clifford, George Ball, McGeorge Bundy, Averell Harriman, Nicholas Katzenbach, Roswell Gilpatrick, Henry Kissinger, Sol Linowitz, John McCloy, John McCone, David Packard, William P. Rogers, and James Schlesinger.

72. See Appendix F.

73. Remarks of the President in an Address to the Nation, Office of the White House Press Secretary, 1 October 1979 (Appendix E).

74. *New York Times*, 23 September 1979 (op. cit., note 68).

75. That the administration was considering some type of overture to Peking as one of a number of "countermeasures" was reported by James Reston in the *New York Times*, 23 September 1979. In his overview, "Cuban Crisis Mishandled" (*Washington Post*, 16 October 1979), Don Oberdorfer mentions Secretary Brown's planned trip to China as well as the fact that the news of the trip was leaked to the press.

76. "Carter's Speech Doesn't Satisfy Senators," *Miami Herald*, 2 October 1979, 13–A.

77. *New York Times Magazine*, 23 October 1979.

Chapter Eight: Conclusion

78. "Long is Opposing SALT Pact, Citing Soviet Bad Faith," *Washington Post*, 13 September 1979.

79. "Soviet Troops in Cuba Treading Heavily on SALT Prospects," *Washington Post*, 27 September 1979, A14.

80. *U.S. News and World Report*, 12 November 1979, p. 12.

81. "Out of the Closet," *New York Times*, 18 September 1979, A25.

82. *Washington Post*, 16 October 1979 (op. cit., note 5).

83. Don Oberdorfer, *Washington Post*, 6 September 1979, A12.

84. Don Oberdorfer, "A Small Soviet Brigade and Its Large Implications," *Washington Post*, 23 September 1979, A2.

85. "Soviet-Cuban Issue Clouds U.S. Tie," *Washington Post*, 29 September 1979, A1–A16.

EDITOR: Nancy Ann Miller
BOOK DESIGNER: Matthew Williamson
JACKET DESIGNER: Matthew Williamson
PRODUCTION COORDINATOR: Harriet Curry
TYPEFACE: Linotron Times Roman and Serifa Light
COMPOSITOR: J. Jarrett Engineering

DAVID D. NEWSOM is a former Under Secretary and Assistant Secretary of State and served as U.S. Ambassador to Libya, Indonesia, and the Philippines. He is currently the Associate Dean of the School of Foreign Service and Director of the Institute for the Study of Diplomacy at Georgetown University, Washington, D.C.